Survivi   t

& Development

Conflict and Social Change Series

Series Editors
Scott Whiteford and William Derman
Michigan State University

Surviving Drought and Development: Ariaal Pastoralists of Northern Kenya, Elliot Fratkin

Harvest of Want: Hunger and Food Security in Central America and Mexico, edited by Scott Whiteford and Anne E. Ferguson

Singing with Sai Baba: The Politics of Revitalization in Trinidad, Morton Klass

Struggling for Survival: Workers, Women, and Class on a Nicaraguan State Farm, Gary Ruchwarger

The Spiral Road: Change in a Chinese Village Through the Eyes of a Communist Party Leader, Huang Shu-min

Kilowatts and Crisis: Hydroelectric Power and Social Dislocation in Eastern Panama, Alaka Wali

Deep Water: Development and Change in Pacific Village Fisheries, Margaret Critchlow Rodman

FORTHCOMING

The Bushman Myth: The Making of a Namibian Underclass, Robert J. Gordon

Computers and Culture: New Information Technology and Social Change in England, David Hakken and Barbara Andrews

Sickness, Health, and Gender in Rural Egypt, Soheir A. Morsy

Literacy and People's Power in a Mozambican Factory, Judith Marshall

The Myth of the Male Breadwinner: Women, Industrialization, and State Policy in the Caribbean, Helen I. Safa

Surviving Drought

& Development

Ariaal Pastoralists of Northern Kenya

Elliot Fratkin

Routledge
Taylor & Francis Group

NEW YORK AND LONDON

First published in paperback 2024

First published 1991 by Westview Press, Inc.

Published 2019 by Routledge
605 Third Avenue, New York, NY 10158

and by Routledge
4 Park Square, Milton Park, Abingdon, Oxon OX14 4RN

Routledge is an imprint of the Taylor & Francis Group, an informa business

Library of Congress Cataloging-in-Publication Data
Fratkin, Elliot M.
   Surviving drought and development : Ariaal pastoralists of
northern Kenya / Elliot Fratkin.
      p. cm.
   Includes bibliographical references and index.
   ISBN 0-8133-7784-6
   . 1. Ariaal (African people)—Social conditions. 2. Ariaal (African
people)—Domestic animals. 3. Ariaal (African people)—Missions.
4. Herders—Kenya—Lewogoso Lukumai Settlement. 5. Rural
development—Kenya—Lewogoso Lukumai Settlement—International
cooperation. 6. Droughts—Kenya—Lewogoso Lukumai Settlement.
7. Lewogoso Lukumai Settlement (Kenya)—Social conditions.
8. Lewogoso Lukumai Settlement (Kenya)—Economic conditions.
I. Title.
DT433.545.A75F73   1991
967.62—dc20   91-22456
                                                                                      CIP

Publisher's Note
The publisher has gone to great lengths to ensure the quality of this reprint but points out that some
imperfections in the original copies may be apparent.

ISBN: 978-0-367-30473-7 (pbk)
ISBN: 978-0-367-28927-0 (hbk)
ISBN: 978-0-429-30802-4 (ebk)

DOI: 10.4324/9780429308024

To the Ariaal of Lewogoso
and to pastoral people everywhere

Contents

Tables and Illustrations

Acknowledgments

This book is the result of research I began in the 1970s and continue to undertake in the 1990s. *Surviving Drought and Development* is a description of how Ariaal pastoralists of northern Kenya have adapted to the vicissitudes of drought, the impact of Western missionaries, and the advent of international development projects, while continuing to maintain their distinctive livestyle and productive economy. When I first lived with the Ariaal from 1974 to 1976, they had only just emerged from a protracted drought (related to the Sahelian Drought of the 1970s) and were rebuilding their domestic herds of camels, cattle, and small stock of goats and sheep, which they depend on for milk, meat, and trade.

When I returned ten years later in 1985, the Ariaal were recovering from an even more severe drought, the Ethiopian Famine of 1982–1984. By this time, however, the formerly isolated area of Marsabit District was inundated with Western relief agencies, including Catholic and Protestant missions as well as international development projects including the UNESCO Integrated Project in Arid Lands. Despite efforts by these agencies encouraging local pastoralists to settle near permanent towns, the Ariaal continue to lead a pastoral lifestyle, subsisting off their livestock in semi-nomadic settlements and trading surplus animals for grains, clothes, and other commodities.

The story of the Ariaal stands in marked contrast to the sad depictions of Africa played out in the Western media, particularly the stories of famine, war, and AIDS. Although these problems are genuine and merit our compassion and intervention, there are other examples from Africa, examples of self-reliance and survivorship, that also demand our attention. The Ariaal represent an African society whose members can thrive and support themselves, particularly if they are given appropriate aid that is of benefit to the pastoral community. The Ariaal have adapted to the arid regions of northern Kenya and will continue to live in these deserts if allowed to keep their animals and maintain production through selective improvements in veterinary care, livestock marketing, and social services.

There are many people in Kenya, Europe, Japan, and the United States who contributed to my research, both directly in Kenya or indirectly through valuable discussions elsewhere.

In Kenya I wish to thank my friends, assistants, and collaborators in Ariaal and Rendille, particularly Larian Aliaro, Anna Marie Aliaro, Kawap

Bulyar, Andrew Dabalen, Lekati Leaduma, Kanikis Leaduma, Joseph Lekuton, Singida Lekuton, Kilecho Lendiyo, Lugi Lengesen, Padamu Lengesen, Nkurso Lengesen, Kitoip Lenkiribe, Matthew Mosian, and Patrick Ngoley.

My thanks to the Institute of African Studies at the University of Nairobi, and in particular to Dr. Gideon Were and George Mathu for their assistance and cooperation while I was a visiting research associate, and to the Office of the President, Republic of Kenya, for their kind permission to conduct research in Kenya.

My appreciation to the researchers and staff of the Integrated Project in Arid Lands (IPAL), and particularly Dr. Walter J. Lusigi and Mr. George Njiru, for their generous assistance and cooperation in my research. This book would not be possible without the copious data collected by IPAL on the ecology and environment of western Marsabit District.

I wish to thank the missionaries in Kenya who showed my family much kindness and hospitality, and who shared their knowledge of the region and discussed their missions: Dale and Suzanne Beverley, Charles and Doris Barnett, and Tim Ryder of the African Inland Church in Marsabit District; Father George Padinjaraparampil, the late Father Peter Morruzzi, Father Redento, and the sisters of the Don Bosco Mission at Korr; and Nick and Lynne Swanepoel of the Summer Institute of Linguistics in Korr.

There are many researchers working in Kenya whose discussions and friendships proved most valuable over the course of my research: Anne Beaman, John and Sharon Berntsen, John and Barbara Galaty, Anders and Meta Grum, Ivan Karp, Naomi and David Kipury, Corrine Kratz, Michael and Judy Rainy, Eric A. Roth, Franz Rottland, Shųn Sato, Gunther Schlee, H. Jurgen Schwartz, Sabine Schwartz, Neal Sobania, Paul Spencer, Steinar Sundvoll, Thomas Spear, Jiro Tanaka, Richard Waller, David and Joan Wiseman, and countless others who shared my interests and enthusiasm.

My special thanks to my severe and scrupulous readers, Patricia Lyons Johnson, Eric A. Roth, Neal Sobania, and Thomas Spear, who let me get away with little (but always in good humor); to Roy Edelfelt and Margo Johnson, who offered many useful suggestions; to Marnie Gwyther, who assisted in the library research (sorry we killed the sunspots); and Eve Anderson, who performed the computer graphics including the wonderful Autocad maps. I am grateful to the editors at Westview, particularly Kellie Masterson, Ellen McCarthy, and not the least William Derman, co-editor with Scott Whiteford of the Conflict and Social Change series, who provided incisive and timely reviews of the manuscript at various stages of preparation.

Finally, I wish to thank my wife, Marty Nathan, and daughter Leah for their unfailing encouragement, collaboration, and companionship (and thanks to Leah for finishing the bibliography after my eyes gave out). I extend a special thanks to my late father, Ralph Fratkin, and my family, Millie, Jake, Arlene, and Susan, for their love and support through the years of my anthropological travels.

There are several institutions that supported the research to which I am very grateful: the Committee for Research and Exploration of the National

Geographic Society for their research grant (No. 3056-85), the Social Science Research Council jointly with the American Council of Learned Societies for their award of an International Doctoral Fellowship in African Studies, the Smithsonian Institution for their support grant while in the field in 1975, and to Penn State University for their research grant in 1990.

Elliot Fratkin
State College, PA

The Possibility of Survival

1 This is an optimistic book, in spite of its central theme of drought and hunger in Africa. The Ariaal of Kenya represent a possibility for African societies, the possibility that a pastoralist people living in the dry margins of the Sahara can feed themselves and maintain their socio-cultural system, even in the face of ecologic, economic, and political dislocations. The Ariaal face pressures on their land, the lure of town life and markets, and, as we shall explore in this book, the active interference of missions and international development agencies on their economy and food production system. Yet the Ariaal continue to live with their large herds of camels, cattle, goats and sheep and to maintain their distinctive way of life. They have incorporated some of the changes around them, including education, health care, and marketing opportunities in the towns, but they have not abandoned their pastoral production system. Their society is resilient and strong.

The story of the Ariaal contradicts the image westerners are exposed to in the media of Africans as helpless victims, the "starving ribcages" one sees in the famine camps. While the scenes of starvation are real enough, particularly in war-torn countries such as Ethiopia and Sudan, the situation of the Ariaal as an active and robust society is far more typical of Africa as a whole. The story of the Ariaal is one of an Africa which too few westerners know.

Ariaal are a small population of approximately 7000 people who subsist on the milk, meat, and trade of their domestic animals in Marsabit District, Kenya's largest, most arid, and least populated region. Because of the arid climate, people of northern Kenya practice little agriculture and the majority are livestock pastoralists including the Turkana (population 248,000), Samburu (70,000), Gabra (30,000), Boran (30,000), Rendille (15,000), Somali (200,000) and Ariaal. The Maasai (350,000), to whom Ariaal are distantly related, are cattle herders who occupy the broad savanna grasslands to the south on the border of Kenya and Tanzania. Pastoralists constitute less than one million of Kenya's twenty five million people; they are a relatively disempowered population in a country predominately made up of settled agriculturalists and urban dwellers.

I lived with one Ariaal community—Lewogoso Lukumai—for nearly two years in 1974–1976. In 1985 I returned to see how the Ariaal fared following

1

the severe drought of 1982–1984, the period of the Ethiopian famine. During my first research in the 1970s, Marsabit District was very isolated with few social services; there were only a handful of schools and dispensaries located in towns built around police posts and Christian missions.

When I returned in 1985, northern Kenya had became a locus of famine-relief efforts and international development projects. Over one half of the pastoral Rendille of Marsabit District had settled in or around small mission towns and famine-relief centers, living on grains distributed primarily by the Catholic Relief Services, or seeking paid work as herders, watchmen, or government employees. The Ariaal continued to live with their animals and had not settled to a large degree in the town centers. The Ariaal, however, were affected by the arrival of a large multi-national development project in their area, the UNESCO Integrated Project in Arid Lands (IPAL). IPAL had descended on the Ariaal area like a storm, building roads, holding livestock auctions, conducting aerial surveys, and encouraging the Ariaal and Rendille to sell more livestock.

When I returned for a brief visit in 1990, the region had undergone an irreversible change. Permanent towns now existed at locations which had previously been only camel watering holes. Many Rendille and some Ariaal children were in school, their older brothers and sisters working for government agencies or private employers. But Ariaal still continued their pastoral existence, living with their animals at some distance from the towns, visiting towns to buy commodities or trade livestock, but otherwise resistant to the large changes that had occurred in their region.

It is a theme of this book that while the ecological processes of drought may lead to hunger and famine for African pastoralists, it is the activities of the development and famine-relief projects themselves which threaten the long-term ability of pastoralists to survive and feed themselves in arid lands.

It is not my view that "development is bad," or that the Ariaal lived in a pristine unblemished state before the arrival of Europeans. The Ariaal, as all African populations, have a long history of contact with other societies, economies, and political forces. Ariaal suffered warfare, smallpox, and famine in the last century, and recent developments in health care, education, and physical security have immensely improved the quality of life, as Ariaal will readily attest.

What I wish to argue is that often the development policies of western agencies, both governmental and non-governmental, are inappropriate and potentially disastrous to their recipients. A major objective of the UNESCO-IPAL project was to destock the pastoral herds and restrict the pastoral range; these policies would directly weaken the ability of Ariaal to adequately feed their households. The policies of the Catholic Church of Marsabit District aimed to settle pastoralists in towns, even though there were not enough resources around the missions to keep their livestock. Neither IPAL nor the Catholic Church considered the fact that the Ariaal's pastoral system is the consequence of generations of adaptation to this arid environment,

Map 1.1 Location of Ariaal

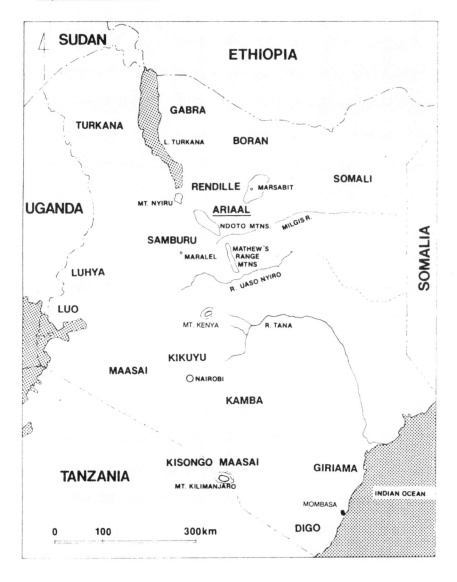

Ariaal women prepare to fetch water on a loading camel at Lewogoso

and that there are few alternatives to supporting human populations in this region outside of livestock pastoralism. This book is an argument for development planners to appreciate the Ariaal's pastoral way of life, by understanding their history, economy, and social organization, and to implement policies that would improve, rather than destroy, their livestock production system.

Living with the Ariaal

I came to live with the Ariaal quite by accident. I originally intended to research the isolated tribes of the Omo River in southwest Ethiopia, and in 1974 had driven on a small motorcycle from Nairobi to the lowland deserts of Marsabit District bordering Ethiopia. When I reached Marsabit town, I discovered there had been a coup against Haile Selassie in Ethiopia and that the border was now closed. Forlorn and dejected, I sat in a dusty bar wondering what I was going to do. It had taken me three days of exhaustive driving to reach Marsabit, maneuvering my bike through sand traps and corrugated ruts, dealing with flat tires and a temperamental battery. I was not anxious to return to Nairobi.

Marsabit is an unusual town in that it lies on a large volcanic mountain standing alone in the desert. At an altitude of over 1500 meters, it is covered in deep and lush tropical forest. This mountain in the desert is home to some of Kenya's largest elephants, and Marsabit boasts a lodge catering to expensive game park tourists arriving by Range Rover or airplane. A boy about fourteen years old, eager for some tourist revenues of his own, approached me in the bar and asked if I would like to see the elephants in the reserve. When I told him no thanks, he thought a minute and asked, "Would you like to see traditional African dances?"

When I told him this would interest me more than seeing elephants, he directed me on the motorcycle to his village, which lay about ten kilometers south of town on the main road. Singida was from Karare village, a large cattle-keeping Ariaal community on Marsabit Mountain. There was indeed dancing going on, but I could see right away this was not a show for the tourists. Several hundred warriors were dancing in a tight circle, their spears twirling in the air and their long braided hair snapping as they jumped-dance. A short man dressed in a long green robe, different from the other elders who were dressed in red or white, was marking the warriors with yellow powder on their shoulders and foreheads. We had arrived in the middle of a serious ritual that lasted several days. I found out later that the warriors of Lorokushu clan, which included most of Karare settlement, were repeating an important *mugit* age-set ritual, the *"mugit* of the name." This ritual was being repeated because the age-set leader (*laiguenani*) had been killed the previous week when he tried to separate a fight between two warriors. This was a serious and unfortunate accident which threatened the health of the entire age-set. The small man in green was a *loibon* medicine man, and he was protecting the warriors from future misfortune with his ritual medicine.

After spending a few days in Karare, drinking milk with the warriors and visiting the cattle camps in the forest, I decided these were people I wanted to live with and study. I knew of other graduate students in anthropology who had miserable experiences in the field, living with people they did not particularly like. I was determined to avoid that fate. My luck was good; the *loibon* medicine-man, Lekati Leaduma, who had supervised the *mugit* ceremony, invited me to accompany him to his friend Lugi Lengesen's settlement in the lowlands, Lewogoso Lukumai. I jumped at the chance. I remained in Lewogoso for the next two years, becoming the adopted son of Leaduma and good friend to Lugi Lengesen. I have never regretted it.

Lewogoso in 1975 was a large settlement of over 250 people. Her animal enclosures held more than 600 camels, 800 cattle, and 2000 goats and sheep. The settlement was located in the desert about fifteen kilometers from Ngurunit in the Ndoto Mountains, a beautiful area of sharp volcanic mountains that rise along Kenya's Rift Valley. Most Ariaal communities are located near or in the mountains, using the highland forests to graze their cattle and rivers to water their human and animal populations. But camels prefer the dry desert, and those Ariaal communities with large camel herds, such as Lewogoso, build their settlements close to, but not within, the mountains. Lewogoso lived on the milk of their camels, the meat of the small stock, and the sale of their cattle.

I was given my own house at Lewogoso, a round dome made of long bent wood covered in mats woven from sisal fiber, and lined on the inside with cattle hides. My house was located between that of Lugi's first wife on one side, and the *loibon* Leaduma's on the other. Initially I used interpreters, such as Singida who accompanied me to Lewogoso, but over time I learned to speak Samburu, a Maasai dialect and one of two languages the Ariaal speak (the other language is Rendille).

After one year, Lugi told me, "You have lived with us a long time now. You have your own goats, you drink milk with us, and you have suffered through the drought with us. Now you are one of us."

While I was a considered part of the community, my status was a bit ambiguous. I was unmarried and considered a member of the warrior age-set, but unlike a warrior who lived with his age-mates outside the village "in the bush" with the cattle, I lived in the settlement like a married elder. The Ariaal were very tolerant of this identity crisis, and laughed good-naturedly when I responded to their question of whether I was an elder or a warrior, "When the elders are eating meat in the settlement, I am an elder; when the warriors are eating meat in the bush, I am a warrior."

When I returned in 1985 I was accompanied by my wife, Marty Nathan, and six-year daughter Leah. Other anthropologists have remarked on the advantages (and disadvantages) of having one's family along, and these applied to us. My status as a married elder was now secure, allowing me access to the men's shade tree for extensive conversations about livestock and the complexities of Ariaal life. Moreover, the experiences and interactions of Marty and Leah gave me insights into the society that I did not have before. Marty, as a physician and volunteer with the Kenya Expanded Program for Immunizations, spent much of her time in the mission clinics in 1985; in 1990 she carried out an extensive research project on health and nutrition of women and children. Both experiences were invaluable to the research and to our relationship with the Ariaal.

Pastoralism: An Adaptation to Arid Lands

Livestock pastoralism is a food production system in which a human community relies on domestic livestock—cattle, camels, goats, sheep (or in Europe and Asia, reindeer, horses, or sheep)—for basic subsistence in the form of milk, meat, blood, and the market sale of stock to purchase other foods, particularly grains. Pastoralism is distinguished from livestock ranching by the fact that herds are taken to pasture and water, rather than having grass brought to them, and by the fact that human herders rely on their animals primarily for milk rather than for beef or sale. As a food production system for the subsistence of the household group (rather than mainly commercial production for the market), the goal of pastoralism is to produce adequate milk, meat and blood for their households' diet, build up numbers of breeding females to insure against loss, and produce enough animals for trade as well as social obligations such as bridewealth, ritual consumption, and stock alliances.

Few pastoral communities live exclusively on livestock products, and they supplement their milk and meat diet with grains, tea, and sugar (purchased by the sale or trade of animals, skins, milk, meat, or cheese), particularly when milk supplies are low. Many groups such as the Karimojong of Uganda or Gogo of Tanzania combine dryland horticulture with livestock keeping. Pastoral societies also vary in their degree of *nomadism*, their disposition to move both homesteads and herds in search of pastures. Some pastoral groups including the Maasai, Samburu, and Ariaal of Kenya live in semi-sedentary settlements, herding their animals in areas around the homestead or taking their animals to seasonal grazing camps during extended drought. Other groups such as the Tarasheq (Tuareg) and Fulbe (Fulani) of the West Africa Sahel are more fully nomadic, moving the entire human and livestock population hundreds of miles in seasonal migrations to the south and north.[1]

Drought and famine are new to neither Ariaal nor other African pastoralists in the arid regions around the Sahara Desert. Drought is caused by the periodic absence of rainfall, and is a chronic feature of Africa's arid regions. Pastoral populations have adapted to arid lands and periodic drought through a variety of mechanisms, including use of animal breeds that can survive on poor vegetation and scattered water resources (such as camels or zebu cattle), and the ability to move animals and people to locations where rain has temporarily fallen. Mobility is perhaps the most important of the nomad's options, when individuals, households, or entire communities move their herds and people to areas of better, if temporary, grazing resources. The ability to move is based in part on ecological factors which determine where households can find grazing, water, and salt resources. But more importantly, the ability to move to new areas depends on maintaining extensive social ties to people living in distant areas related by marriage, descent group ties, or personal friendships cemented by years of exchanging stock and favors.

Unfortunately many of these safety mechanisms have broken down in the past thirty years. Loss of pastoral lands to population pressures (of both humans and livestock), encroachment on important grazing areas by expanding agricultural or other pastoral groups, as well as the creation of commercial ranches and game parks have all contributed to a growing restriction of grazing lands for many pastoral groups.

Furthermore, the policies of both local governments and international donor agencies in many African countries have largely encouraged pastoralists to settle. In countries such as Kenya where government administrators are largely made up of people from agricultural rather than pastoralist backgrounds, livestock pastoralism is viewed as primitive, unproductive, wasteful. The idea of people moving their houses with their animals, distant from town resources, and living in unsafe conditions is abhorrent to many sedentary agricultural populations. Because of their low population densities and geographical isolation pastoralists tend to be marginalized politically and underrepresented in government decision-making. The need for foreign revenues led the Kenyan government to expand national game parks and prohibit pastoralists from grazing their animals, and the demand for beef for the growing urban populations led to government policies encouraging pastoralists to sell more livestock in commercial markets.

The integration of pastoralists into the cash market is not new but a process that has occurred over several generations. All Ariaal households sell some livestock each year to purchase foods (particularly maizemeal called *posho*, tea and sugar) and household goods (cooking utensils, plates and cups, sheets, shoes, and beads for jewelry). More recently, however there has emerged a class of livestock entrepreneurs who buy and sell livestock on the commercial market. In some areas such as Samburu and Maasailand, individual entrepreneurs have gained title to private ranches, and poorer pastoralists find themselves excluded from pasture that was formerly shared. Denied access to grazing lands, these poorer pastoralists are forced to sell their animals to buy food, and ultimately become further impoverished as stockless migrants to towns. A polarization of haves and have-nots is emerging in some pastoral regions, not so much between agriculturalists and pastoralists as among pastoralists themselves.

But pastoralists persist, to use Peter Rigby's[2] phrase, primarily because, I believe, given adequate pasture, physical security and access to markets, pastoralists have a reliable way to produce food in an arid and variable environment, through wet and season and dry, good year and bad. Current development activities including the increased participation of pastoralists in the market and the growth of small towns offer new advantages as well as new risks.

Ariaal: Surviving Drought and Development

Drought is a climatic problem, the prolonged absence of rains, and is a recurring feature of Africa's climate.[3] Famine however is a severe economic and political dislocation when people do not have enough food and face massive starvation. While drought does not always lead to famine, drought and famine are often interlinked in Africa's arid zones. The 20th century has seen three major famines in northeastern Africa, in 1913–1914, 1968–1974, and 1982–1984. Yet the periods between 1900–1930 and 1950–1959 were unusually wet; mean rainfall recorded in the Sahel in the 1950's was nearly double that recorded between 1968–1985, which showed an unprecedented seventeen years of rainfall decline.[4] Clearly meteorological drought is a recurring and periodic phenomenon in Africa, or as Michael Glantz writes, "a part of climate and not apart from it".[5]

Ariaal have experienced drought (and to a lesser extent famine) throughout their remembered history. People still recall the bitter period in the late 19th century, remembered as *emutai* (the disaster) when pastoral peoples throughout Kenya experienced livestock epidemics, smallpox, war, drought, and famine.

Prior to the 1970s, Ariaal and other pastoralists faced the problems of drought by a variety of means including mobility, herd diversity, or taking up alternative economies. Since the early 1970's however Kenyan pastoralists have increasing relied on famine-relief aid provided by international relief services including USAID and private Christian missions. This shift occurred

Ukarre Lengesen with two newborn camels, Lewogoso settlement

primarily because of the expansion of mission services and growth of towns after Kenyan Independence in 1963. Much of the food aid to pastoralists continued after the crises had passed, however, and contributed to the concentrated settling of Rendille and Turkana pastoralists in northern Kenya during the 1980s.

Ariaal have not settled at the mission towns to the same extent as the Rendille, but have continued to subsist on their herds, selling an average offtake of 5–7% of their animals annually. An Ariaal elder once remarked,

"We will never settle down in places like Korr. While it's true their medicines and shops are good things, we prefer to move with our animals, to live with our animals and drink their milk every day, and not be forced to eat *posho* (maizemeal porridge) like old people every day."

A major question of this study is why have Ariaal continued their pastoral economy despite pressures from development agencies, Christian missions, and government ministries to settle down. The answer is found in part in the economic and ecologic factors of livestock production, where Ariaal live close to mountain resources that enable them to graze their cattle and small stock at some distance from the lowland mission centers in the camel-keeping areas. The Ariaal's tripartite dependence on cattle, camels and small stock, as well as their flexible allocation of herding labor force, has afforded Ariaal more maneuverability, mobility, and survivorship than the Rendille.

Moreover, the Ariaal have a history of self-reliance, surviving through recurring drought by utilizing their ties of kinship, marriage, and friendship to the allied Samburu and Rendille to herd their animals over a wide area, and to defend their settlements from competing Turkana and Boran pastoralists.

It remains to be seen whether the Ariaal can withstand the large scale famine-relief efforts and development projects which have descended on their area, particularly efforts by the religious missions and the international development community to settle the pastoralists down.

The Mission Towns

Northern Kenya was neglected under British rule except as a military buffer against Ethiopia and rival European powers in northeast Africa. Following Kenyan independence, western Christian missions flocked to the north as the government welcomed their efforts to build schools, dispensaries, and roads. The Catholic Church and the Protestant evangelical African Inland Church (AIC) had been denied much influence in Kenya under the British (who preferred Anglican and Presbyterian missions), and they were eager to expand their activities in an independent Kenya.

Both the AIC and Catholic Church built their missions at permanent water sites, usually small towns with a police post and a few shops. The Catholics built missions at Archer's Post, Laisamis, and Marsabit town, the Protestants at Logologo, Mt. Kulal, and Ngurunit. These towns grew as the missions' schools, dispensaries, and employment attracted new residents.

It was the famine of the early 1970s however that led to large scale settling of pastoralists in the mission towns. Although this famine was precipitated by drought (the same drought that contributed to the famine in the West African Sahel), the famine in Marsabit District was aggravated largely by the political disruptions of the 1960s, when dissident Muslim populations in northeastern Kenya attempted to secede and join Somalia. The insurgency, known as *shifta* (meaning "bandits"), was characterized by the government imprisoning Somali and Boran people and confiscating their animals, leading to widespread stock raising by the Boran against neutral Rendille and Ariaal peoples. Rendille moved close to the missions for physical security, and many lost their animals to the drought and raids.

During the 1970s and into the 1980s, the Catholic missions undertook much of the famine-aid distribution in the district. New missions were developed among the Rendille at Korr and Kargi, and food aid in the form of maize, soy, and powdered milk were distributed to thousands of impoverished pastoralists. The missions continued to distribute the food aid long after the drought had passed, however, leading to a wide spread settling of Rendille around the missions at Korr, Kargi, and Laisamis. Meanwhile, other church groups assisted pastoralists to seek alternative techniques of food production. The National Council of Churches of Kenya (NCCK) introduced irrigated maize (corn) farming for poor Rendille and Boran on Marsabit Mountain, and AIC missionaries began animal restocking programs, offering poor pastoralists goats and camels in the 1980s.

The Ariaal did not move into the mission centers in large numbers, although a few divided their households so that one wife and some children could live near the mission, and the other wife and children remain to herd animals. Ariaal are generalists in their food production strategy, and see the missions as one more resource to utilize in a hazardous and unpredictable environment. The mission towns are recognized as an alternative to pastoral life, particularly for poor households who have few animals. Furthermore, they are seen as essential centers to gain employment, sell livestock, seek health care, and obtain educations for children. Where Ariaal men prefer to herd their animals and live at some distance from the towns, Ariaal women find life in the town more secure and easier to live in.

A Lewogoso woman living in the AIC mission town of Ngurunit said,

"I like living here at Ngurunit. There is no water in Lewogoso, no place to buy food. Besides my husband has a new wife to take care of him and he doesn't need me now. When my cows are here, I can sell the milk and buy what I want. When we keep some of our goats here, I can sell them too. Now that its dry I cannot keep these animals here, but I will bring them here when it rains. Now I cook for the school teacher's wife and watch their children, and they pay me some money. If my husband tells me to go to Lewogoso, I will tell him I won't go. He will agree because he knows it is drought there and he can't feed all of us. Anyway, he would prefer to take his new young wife. He can't do anything bad to me if I refuse because I have enough animals, and according to our custom he can't take my animals from me. I have my own animals and my own children to herd them. So who needs hardship in the bush (*ngoloto ti awulo*)?"[6]

Town life offers new opportunities for the Ariaal, particularly for those people who do not own enough animals to support themselves from pastoralism. To the Ariaal, towns represent one more option of survival in a land of very scarce resources.

The UNESCO-IPAL Project

The Ariaal in the 1970s had their hands full, coping with drought, fending off armed raiders during *shifta* time, and adjusting to the growth of the mission towns, when a new force, one quite alien to their previous experience, descended on their region. For ten years between 1976 and 1985, the UNESCO-IPAL project conducted research and implemented development schemes aimed at conserving the land. From headquarters in Marsabit and a large base camp in Ngurunit, IPAL developed livestock auctions, built roads, and ran commercial shops selling household goods, all of which were designed to encourage Ariaal and Rendille to sell more livestock and reduce their herd sizes.

The IPAL project originated in 1976 when UNESCO (the United Nations Scientific, Educational, and Cultural Organization) and the newly formed UNEP (United Nations Environment Program) held an International Conference on Desertification in Nairobi. Scientists and scholars assembled to make sense of what happened in the Sahel, when tens of thousands of people died during the drought of 1968–1973. The Integrated Project in Arid Lands (IPAL) emerged as a positive program to integrate basic research on "desertification," the physical expansion of desert regions, and practical policies involving training and demonstrations that would improve humans' use of the arid environments. It was decided to build a pilot IPAL project in Marsabit District, with later IPAL projects in Tunisia, Sudan, and the Mideast.

A predominant view at the Conference on Desertification was that the environmental degradation of arid lands was caused largely by human mismanagement and overpopulation. Pastoralists themselves were held responsible for the desert moving south through their practices of maximizing herd sizes and overgrazing an already fragile environment.[7]

This position, which some environmentalists still hold[8], adheres both to the "tragedy of the commons" view that people do not take care of resources jointly shared between them[9], and the theories of Thomas Malthus (1766–1834) who proposed that populations increase faster than their food supply. These populations are periodically reduced by "famine, pestilence, war, and plague."[10] Africa experienced large population growth in the 1950s as health care had led to declining mortality, while fertility remained high. A modern day Malthusian, Paul Ehrlich, writes, "whatever problem exists on earth, its origins begin with overpopulation."[11]

Certainly both human and livestock populations have increased in Africa. In 1950 Africa had 219 million people and 295 million livestock; by 1990 populations had grown to 660 million humans and over 600 million livestock, with annual growth rates jumping from 1.5% in 1950 to 3–4% in 1990. The total fertility rate (the average number of births per woman) in Africa is 6.9 (compared to 1.8 in the United States).

Compounding this problem, food production has grown at only one half the rate of the population; per capita grain production for the continent declined from 180 kg in 1950 to less than 100 kg in 1990 at a time when grain production increased in every other continent. It is estimated that one quarter or 150 million people in Africa are hungry or malnourished.[12]

A problem with the view that overpopulation is the cause of famine is that, on the whole, Africa is not overpopulated. Areas where populations are very crowded (large cities and certain countries including Nigeria and Rwanda) are not those which suffered from the famines of 1970's and 1980's. The regions which suffered the famines, those of the Sahel and Sudan, have among the *lowest* population densities on the continent. Furthermore the most densely populated countries in the world, India and China, have been self sufficient in grain production for several decades. As described by the economist Amartya Sen, the problem of hunger is not one of food shortage, but access to food. Hunger is caused by poverty, not food availability.[13]

This point is driven home in a study of the Sahelian drought, *The Seeds of Famine*. Authors Franke and Chasin argue that British and French colonialism planted the "seeds of famine" in West Africa by encouraging, through coercive taxation policies, the cash-cropping of ground nuts (peanuts) and cotton in the Sahel. As commercial growers expanded their estates, poor farmers were forced north onto arid pastoral lands, pushing the local pastoralists off their dry season grazing lands. When ecological disaster occurred with the drought of 1968–73, the pastoralists could no longer use their dry season lands and faced massive starvation.[14]

The Conference on Desertification in Nairobi did not discuss political or economic causes of famine, but focused on climatic issues, overpopulation and human mismanagement. From its inception at the conference, IPAL viewed the pastoral practices of the local Ariaal and Rendille as responsible for environmental degradation, particularly their practice of maximizing their herd size and reluctance to sell or cull their animals.[15] This view of pastoralism as "irrational and wasteful" has a long lineage; it is found in Kenya government documents from the colonial era to today. But as Michael Horowitz writes in an AID evaluation paper on West African livestock projects,

> "So many documents, officials, and even scientists repeat the assertion of pastoral responsibility for environmental degradation that the accusation has achieved the status of a fundamental truth, so self evident a case that marshaling evidence in its behalf is superfluous if not in fact absurd, like trying to satisfy a skeptic that the earth is round or the sun rises in the East."[16]

IPAL's starting point was that pastoralism in Marsabit District was a major factor in the degradation of the environment. Their program aimed to reduce pastoral herd size by encouraging the pastoralists to sell their livestock and take up alternative economy such as wage labor. However, by the end of the IPAL project in 1985, Ariaal and Rendille were selling no more animals than in previous times, and in fact were buying more livestock through the improved market conditions.

IPAL was never able to reduce herd size, primarily because they never understood or appreciated the rationale and productivity of livestock pastoralism in arid regions. Like many other development projects aimed at pastoralists, IPAL never started from the point of determining what was beneficial to the pastoralists. Their starting point were their own interests, conservation in the abstract, without even determining what effect the Ariaal and Rendille had on the environment. Despite the millions of dollars spent by the project, IPAL showed very little interest in interviewing the pastoralists themselves about their economic production system. There were a few IPAL researchers who investigated local pastoral practices, but their suggestions such as low cost improvements in veterinary care or training in husbandry techniques fell on deaf ears and were never implemented. IPAL's objective was simply to remove the inhabitants from the range. Failing to achieve this, IPAL folded by 1986.

Elliot Fratkin and Rendille associates Patrick Ngoley and Larian Aliaro, 1990

Summary

As an anthropologist who has lived and studied the Ariaal for a long time, my principle interest lies in analyzing how this society survives both drought and development. I investigate how the Ariaal maintain their livestock economy in this arid region, and how they cope with the influences of the development projects and the mission activities.

I pose several questions in this study that relate not only to the Ariaal but to pastoral development in general. Can pastoralists truly be self-sufficient? Is self-reliance the same as self-sufficiency? To what degree can pastoralists continue to feed themselves if their herding range in further constricted? How do pastoralists view the market? Can they compete successfully within it? Is settling down around towns necessarily a bad thing? Finally, what constitutes appropriate development in pastoral regions? With what objectives should donor agencies direct their efforts; what projects would benefit the pastoral producer?

This book is organized into several thematic chapters, including the formation of Ariaal identity in the 19th and 20th centuries (Chapter 2), Ariaal livestock production and human nutrition (Chapter 3), settlement structure, household variation, gender inequality and the organization of labor (Chapter 4), the impact of Christian missions distributing famine-relief foods (Chapter 5), and Ariaal interaction with the UNESCO-IPAL development project (Chapter 6). Chapter 7 locates the Ariaal in the larger context of contemporary Kenyan pastoralism, and compares their situation to that of the Maasai, Turkana, and Rendille. The final chapter argues that modernization and development do not necessarily lead to the collapse of indigenous institutions and loss of culture, particularly when development efforts start from the needs of the people they are attempting to serve.

Notes

1. For a variety of perspectives on pastoralism see Dyson-Hudson 1972, 1980; Dyson-Hudson and Dyson-Hudson 1982; Frantz 1980; Galaty 1981a; Goldschmidt 1971; Ingold 1980; Jacobs 1965; Salzman 1971, 1972, 1980; Spooner 1973.
2. Rigby 1985.
3. Drought was recorded in Marsabit District in 1934, 1939, 1942–1945, 1950, 1954–1955, 1965, 1970, 1973, 1976, 1980, 1982–1984, and 1987–88. The causes of drought are complex and yield to no single explanation. Experts have pointed to several meteorological processes that lead to drought including periodic flaring of the sun ("sunspots"), increases in atmospheric dust, the warming of the planet through increased CO_2 and fluorocarbon emissions (the greenhouse effect), and ENSO events in the Pacific Ocean.

ENSO events (the El Nino-Southern Oscillation) are major disturbances in the air pressure and surface temperatures in the Pacific Ocean leading to increased rainfall in the eastern Pacific and South America and extensive drought in the western Pacific, Indian Ocean, and Africa. ENSO events occur roughly every five years; the largest was recorded in 1982/83 and corresponded to the major drought in Ethiopia and the Horn of Africa. The origins of ENSO events are still not clear. For an extensive discussion of meteorological causes of drought in Africa, see Glantz 1987a; 1987b.
4. Nicholson 1979, 1980.
5. Glantz 1987a:38.
6. Interview with Kursa Lengesen, Ngurunit Kenya July 27, 1990.
7. UNEP 1977; Lamprey 1976.
8. The World Watch Institute, an environmental monitoring group, wrote in its 1985 State of the World report, "Africa's plight is rooted in its phenomenal rate of population growth—the fastest of any continent in history. . . . Over population is outstripping the carrying capacity of farmland, while destroying forests and grass-lands." Brown and Wolf 1985:8–9.
9. Hardin 1968.
10. Malthus 1958 (1798).
11. Ehrlich *et al.* 1973:278.
12. Eicher 1986; FAO production Yearbook 1950, 1990.
13. Sen 1981.
14. Franke and Chasin 1980.
15. Lamprey 1983; Lamprey and Yusuf 1981; IPAL 1984.
16. Horowitz 1979:27.

Ariaal: An Identity of Survival

2 The ability of Ariaal to survive the adversities they face today is rooted in their cultural identity forged in the 19th century. Ariaal formed from refugees of several pastoralist societies escaping the drought, famine, and wars of the last century. Their cultural identity is the product of their adaptation to a marginal ecological region by a variety of mechanisms including a mobile division of labor, inter-household cooperation, and an extensive herding strategy utilizing social ties to other societies. These mechanisms which enabled the Ariaal to adapt to the ecological and political adversities of the past continue to serve them in the present as they contend with new social forces and conditions. The Ariaal remain an "opportunity oriented" society, seeking new means of adaptation while retaining older proven methods.

Ariaal are a population of about 7000 who live in pastoral settlements along the base of the Ndoto Mountains and Marsabit Mountain in Marsabit District, northern Kenya. This is an arid region to the east of Kenya's Rift Valley, consisting of low lying desert bordered by high forested mountains. Ariaal are bounded to the west and south by highland Samburu (pop. 70,000), cattle pastoralists related to Maasai, and to the north and east by desert dwelling Rendille (pop. 15,000), camel pastoralists related to Somalis. Related by descent and marriage to both Samburu and Rendille, Ariaal households utilize their kinship ties to graze their cattle, camels, goats and sheep in distant Samburu and Rendille pastures.

Economically, Ariaal are distinguished from Samburu and Rendille by their tripartite production of camels, cattle, and small stock, as opposed to the specialized cattle/small stock production of Samburu and the camel/small stock system of Rendille. Figure 2.1 shows mean ownership of camels, cattle, and small stock among Ariaal and Rendille households. The Ariaal have substantially larger cattle and small stock herds in the 1980s (80.8 and 20.6 respectively compared to 2.6 cattle and 31.7 small stock per Rendille household), although Rendille had larger camel herds per household during the 1970s before the 1982–1984 drought.

The herding regime of Ariaal places large demands on household labor, as cattle must be grazed in the wet highlands while camels prefer the hot

Map 2.1 Location of Ariaal, Samburu, and Rendille

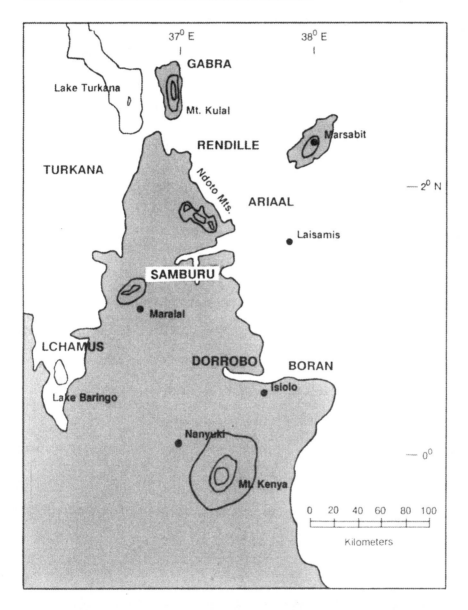

Figure 2.1 Livestock Ownership in Ariaal and Rendille

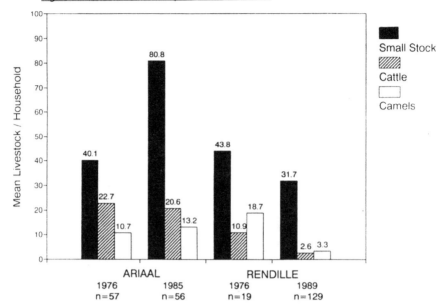

deserts. Ariaal settlements are large, between fifteen and fifty houses, with households cooperating in herding tasks as adolescents and members of the warrior age-set graze non-milking stock in independent camps away from the domestic settlements, cattle in the highlands and camels in the lowlands. The more sedentary settlements remain near permanent water at the base of the mountains, where its residents of married adults and young children subsist off the milk of their camels and meat and trade of their small stock.

The Ariaal's diversity in livestock enables them to survive climatic stress and social upheavals to a greater degree than either Samburu or Rendille. Whereas Samburu families lost up to 75% of their cattle during the 1982/ 84 drought,[1] Ariaal were able to subsist on the milk of their drought-adapted camels and build up their flocks of small stock to trade for cattle during the post-drought recovery. By relying on their cattle for trade and exchange rather than subsistence (as do the Samburu), Ariaal have a large surplus of animals for sale in the marketplace, and are better integrated into the cash marketplace than the Rendille who sell very few camels. Furthermore, their surplus of cattle provides stock for bridewealth payments, and Ariaal men have a higher polygyny rate (1.39) than the Rendille (1.15), as shown in Figure 2.2. The increase in both Ariaal and Rendille polygyny from 1976 to 1985 reflects an increase in cattle ownership and its use in bridewealth exchange in both societies.

The Ariaal's relatives and neighbors, the camel-keeping Rendille, have not fared as well as the Ariaal through the droughts of the 1970s and 1980s. With their herding lands restricted by political instability and government

Figure 2.2 Polygyny Rate in Ariaal and Rendille

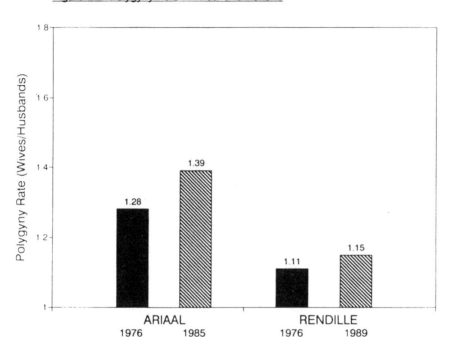

grazing controls, many Rendille were forced to settle around the famine-relief centers where today nearly 50% of the 15,000 Rendille live around the towns of Korr, Kargi, and Laisamis. Ariaal however have been able to maintain their pastoral economy, herding their cattle in the highlands, surplus camels in the lowlands, and subsisting off the milk, meat and trade of their resident camels and small stock in the more sedentary domestic settlements. While a few Ariaal families have moved to the missions at Korr and Ngurunit, they are less than 15% of the total population, and most Ariaal are able to live off the products of their animals.

It remains a question how long the Ariaal can maintain their pastoral lifestyle due to further constrictions of their grazing lands and the attractions of town life. However given land with which to graze and a guarantee of political security, the Ariaal would prefer to remain with their animals, their certain source of livelihood.

Origins of Ariaal in the Nineteenth Century

Ariaal are a recent social formation created by immigrants from Rendille and Samburu (as well as Boran, Dasenech, Maasai, and Turkana) who came together in western Marsabit District during the period of drought, warfare, and disease of the later 19th century. This period, remembered in Samburu and Maasai traditions as the disaster (*emutai*), gave rise to Ariaal society as destitute Rendille and Samburu joined together along the highland/lowland interface of north central Kenya's Rift Valley to subsist off their small stock, camels and cattle.

The history of East African pastoralists is only recently coming to light as scholars piece together evidence from oral traditions, archaeology, and linguistic reconstructions. The Samburu and Rendille come from widely different backgrounds, yet both pastoralist groups have been intermarried and allied for many generations. Samburu are related to Maasai, cattle-keeping Nilotes who entered Kenya from the Sudan sometime in the last one thousand years. The Rendille are Cushitic speakers distantly related to Somali and south Ethiopian peoples who have occupied the arid semi-deserts around Lake Turkana since at least the first millennium A.D.

Proto-Maasai groups moved south as Nilotic Turkana pushed into north-west Kenya, themselves forced south by expanding populations in central Sudan. These Maa speaking groups intermingled with Eastern Cushitic speakers (proto-Somali, Boni, and Rendille), where the Maasai groups borrowed customs from the Cushites including male and female circumcision (clitoridectomy) and very possibly their age-set organization.[2]

By 1800 A.D. the savannas and arid plains of Kenya were occupied by nomadic cattle and camel pastoralists, while agriculturalists occupied the highlands around Mt. Kenya (Kikuyu, Embu, and Meru peoples), the western regions around Lake Victoria (Luyia and Luo peoples), and the Indian Ocean coast (Swahili speaking groups).

During the 19th century pastoral populations were pushing against each other with Turkana from Sudan expelling Samburu and Rendille from the northern plains west of Lake Turkana. To the south, rival Maasai clusters competed for grazing lands, with the Purko and Kisongo Maasai defeating Maa-speaking groups around them including the Uasin Gishu, Laikipia, and Paraguyu.

The fiercest of the internicine Maasai wars occurred between the Laikipiak and the Purko Maasai during the 1870s, when both groups were competing for the rich grazing lands around Lake Naivasha. Maasai traditions hold that the Purko medicine-man (*oloiboni*) named Mbatiany was able to persuade the warriors from the Kisongo Maasai to join the Purko and deal the Laikipiak a total defeat. The Laikipiak were annihilated, and their few survivors assimilated into neighboring Purko, Samburu, and the newly emerging Ariaal communities.[3]

The Samburu and Rendille were only marginally involved in the Laikipiak wars to the south. During the period around 1875, the Samburu pulled away from Turkana raiders and were living in the extreme north on the eastern side of Lake Turkana, near the Dasenech people. The camel-keeping Rendille, firmly allied to the Samburu by intermarriage, occupied the lowland basin of the Chalbi Desert near Mt. Marsabit, fighting those Laikipiak remnants who had fled the Purko Maasai in the south.

Junior elders dancing, Samburu wedding

It is during the Laikipiak Wars that Ariaal are first distinguished from the Rendille in contemporary oral histories, and they are noted for their fierce fighting against the Laikipiak and Kiriman families of Boran, from whom Ariaal captured a large number of camels during the warriorhood period of the Tarigirik age-set (c.1865–1879).[4]

Kenyan pastoralists faced hardship not only from the warfare of the latter 19th century but also from the steady series of diseases, including bovine pleuro-pneumonia in 1882 and rinderpest in 1891 (which devastated cattle herds), followed by smallpox (which decimated human populations). The concentration of Samburu and Rendille populations in the Chalbi Desert west of Mt. Marsabit as a refuge from Laikipiak and Turkana raiders may have led to the rapid spread of disease among their populations in this period.[5] The rinderpest epidemic had mainly effected Samburu and Turkana herds in the north, while the Rendille, relying on camels, were relatively immune to these epizootics. W.A. Chanler, the first European to travel through Rendille territory, reported in 1896 that the Rendille were the only prosperous pastoralists he encountered, while the Samburu he met along the eastern side of the Ndoto Mountains were destitute and eager to exchange donkeys and small stock for cattle of which they possessed very few.[6]

Due to the drought, raids, and epidemics, increasing numbers of Samburu moved east into the Rendille lowlands with their small stock. While the Rendille remained a relatively cohesive group during this period, isolating themselves against Laikipiak and Boran enemies by moving farther into the Chalbi Desert, the Samburu dispersed into many small groups trying to survive by hunting and gathering, raising small stock, or stealing from groups including their allies the Rendille. Describing this period, my adopted Ariaal father, Lekati Leaduma, himself descended from Samburu and Maasai, told me,

> "During the times of *Terito* age-set (1893–1911) after the period of warfare with the Maasai, all the Samburu were living on this side of the Ndoto Mountains. Even my father was living on Marsabit Mountain, keeping both camels and cattle. During this time, and of the *Marikon* age-set (1879–1893) before them, Samburu were poor. When the cattle were finished (by rinderpest), Samburu were living as Dorrobo (poor hunters-gatherers), even eating elephants. Some stole camels from Rendille as thieves (*tombon*), others worked for the Rendille as herdboys, to be paid in small stock, camels, or cattle."

During this period of decimation and disaster in the last decade of the 19th century, many Samburu migrated to Rendille and formed mixed Samburu/Rendille communities of impoverished herders attempting to build up small stock, camels and cattle near the mountain bases. These groups were alternatively called Masagera ("those who follow the Maasai" in Samburu), Turia (Samburu for "mixture"), or Ariaal. The term Ariaal derives from the Boran word for mobile livestock camp (*arjara*) and denoted in the first half of this century those mixed groups of Rendille, Boran, and Samburu who moved with their animals along the mountain bases.[7]

By the beginning of the 20th century the fortunes of the Samburu and the Rendille were to dramatically reverse. The eastward shift of Samburu groups into the Rendille lowlands protected their flocks of small stock and few cattle from Turkana and Laikipiak raiders, and the Samburu and Ariaal were able to steadily rebuild their herds. However smallpox spread to Marsabit District in the 1890's, devastating the Rendille to a greater degree than the Samburu, possibly because the Samburu had had previous exposure during contacts with Swahili caravans from the coast. Concentrated in large populations in the Chalbi and Kaisut Deserts, the Rendille lost an estimated 50% of their people.[8]

By 1900, the former position of strength and superiority of the Rendille in their alliance with the Samburu was lost. The Rendille had large camel-herds but few herders to manage them, and they hired and adopted Samburu and Ariaal labor in exchange for livestock. The Rendille's misfortunes thus became both the Samburu and Ariaal's good fortune, as they were able to build their cattle and small stock herds at a steady rate.

By the end of the nineteenth century, pastoralist groups in northern Kenya were beginning to recover from the disasters of the previous twenty years, with the Samburu rebuilding their cattle herds, and the Rendille slowly recovering from their decimations. The twentieth century saw an expansion of Samburu onto the Loroghi plateau near Maralel (in exchange for white settler occupation of Laikipiak District), and the continuing infringement of Rendille lands by grazing restrictions, Turkana and Boran incursions, and outmigration of Rendille men. The sequence of events and consequences of 20th century colonial policies, drought, and development projects are the subject of the latter half of this book, in Chapters 5, 6, and 7.

Ariaal and the Samburu-Rendille Alliance

Rendille and Samburu have been politically allied for many generations. This alliance, originally described by Paul Spencer in *Nomads in Alliance,* is based both on the noncompetitiveness of their herding strategies (camels graze in lowland deserts while cattle need the water and grasses of the highlands), and the outmigration of Rendille men and women into Samburu society, where poor Rendille men take up cattle production among the Ariaal and Samburu, and polygynous Samburu men marry Rendille women as second wives.

Spencer suggested that the Ariaal were a product of the alliance between Samburu and Rendille, operating as a conduit for Rendille migration in to Samburu. He postulated that the movement of Rendille into Samburu was driven by demographic forces where the Rendille population grew faster than their camel herds. The slow rate of camel reproduction, combined with Rendille inheritance rules of primogeniture that leaves a man's livestock to his eldest son, led to the outmigration of second and third sons into Ariaal and Samburu society to take up cattle and small stock raising. While this model was may have been the norm in the 1950s during Spencer's research, by the 1980s during my fieldwork, Rendille outmigration into Ariaal had declined as they found new opportunities raising cattle or seeking wage work in the growing towns.[9]

Ariaal Identity Today

Where the Ariaal may be the product of a Samburu-Rendille alliance, the Ariaal today see themselves as a distinct society. Ariaal distinguish themselves from Rendille by their raising of cattle as well as camels and small stock, by their speaking Samburu language, and by their incorporation into the Samburu descent system and age-set organization.Yet they are not considered wholly Samburu, as they live in the desert in large Rendille-like settlements, raise camels, are bilingual in Rendille and Samburu, and follow many Rendille customs.

Ariaal woman assembling Rendille-style house

Ariaal identity is consequently ambiguous; they are neither fully Samburu nor Rendille, but a mixture of the two. This is as problematic to Ariaal as it is to outsiders. An Ariaal elder remarked,

> "We're really something in between Samburu and Rendille. We are not something different, we are really both things together. We live in Rendille country, keep camels, and follow camel rites like *soriu* and *almhado*. Although we stay away from the *galgulumi* (Rendille age-set initiation ritual) as we do not think the Rendille want us there, we do send our camels there to be blessed. Our houses are Rendille, and we speak both languages. Yet we also keep cattle, we follow the Samburu *mugit* (age-set rites), and speak in Samburu language. If I was in Nairobi and someone asked me who I was, I would say Samburu. But when I'm in Maralel (the capital of Samburu District), they call me "filthy Rendille," and when I'm in Korr (a Rendille center), they call me Ariaal. But in fact, Lewogoso (an Ariaal and Samburu subclan) and Tubsha (a Rendille clan) are brothers—we came from the same people a long time ago. The younger brothers of Rendille families (i.e. those without camel inheritances) came towards Samburu, or Samburu came down into the lowlands to keep camels; they are now the same people who live in the same country."[10]

There is no "typical" Ariaal community, but rather a continuum in identity from small and isolated Samburu speaking cattle-keeping settlements in the highlands to the large Rendille-type settlements in the lowlands subsisting on camels and small stock. The highland communities on Marsabit Mountain, for example, speak mainly Samburu, trace their descent to Samburu or Laikipiak Maasai ancestors, and view themselves as the most northern group of the Maasai speaking world. These highland communities are similar in appearance to Samburu, whose settlements consist of small circles of three to eight domed houses constructed of heavy timber plastered with mud and cattle dung. These settlements keep mainly cattle and some small stock, all of which are managed by the household labor force.

Lowland Ariaal settlements are much larger and identical in appearance to Rendille villages. Where Samburu houses are low and squat structures designed for warmth in the cool highlands, Rendille houses are large and airy, constructed of woven sisal mats tied onto a portable wooden frame. These houses, shown in Figure 2.3, are designed for protection from heat and wind, and can be easily dismantled to be carried by camel during frequent pastoral movements.

Ariaal culture is also a mixture of Samburu and Rendille elements. Ariaal follow Rendille rituals associated with the well being of the livestock herds including the yearly *almhado* rite in which all camels are blessed, and the more frequent *soriu* ritual, where each household sacrifices a goat or sheep four times during the year. Furthermore, Ariaal settlements, like Rendille but unlike Samburu, have a ritual center called the *na'apo*, a fenced enclosure in the center of the settlement where a ritual fire continuously burns, a feature not found in Samburu. As in Rendille, male Ariaal elders gather every evening in the *na'apo* for prayers, and will bless the settlement's residents from the *na'apo* during the yearly *almhado* rite.[11]

Like Maasai, Samburu, Rendille and other East African pastoralists with segmentary descent organization, Ariaal religion is decentralized—there are no major deities, no ancestor worship, nor are there well established myths of origin or afterlife. Ariaal believe in a supreme being (called *Ngai* in Samburu and *Wakh* in Rendille) which is appealed to in prayers for peace, rain, and fertility, but it is a distant force not directly concerned with affairs on earth. Certain families known as *lais* in Ariaal (*iipire* in Rendille) possess strong blessings (as well as powerful curses), and their members are often called to lead community wide prayers.

Ariaal share certain beliefs and practices with the Samburu which are not found in Rendille, particularly beliefs in sorcery and the power of *loibonok* medicine men. Sorcerers are believed to be neighbors or kin who wish to harm someone due to jealousy or unjust resentments. They use sorcery poisons which are believed to cause unusual diseases such as insanity or blindness, infertility in women, or large scale losses in livestock. If one suspects sorcery, the only protection is to seek the protective medicines of the *loibonok* ritual diviners, medicine men descended from Maasai families living among the Samburu and Ariaal. Being an adopted son of the *loibon* Leaduma, I witnessed several dozen of his curative rituals. I was struck by the degree to which sorcery accusations increased among the more isolated Ariaal communities, particularly those deep in the Ndoto Mountains distant

Figure 2.3 Rendille house construction (Drawing by Anders Grum)

**South
Elevation
1:50**

**Cross
Section
1:50**

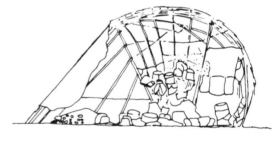

**Plan
1:50**

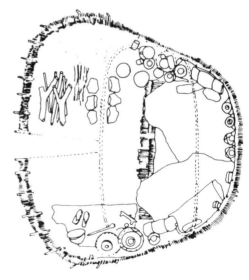

Male elders prepare sheep for slaughter, soriu *ceremony at Lewogoso settlement*

Figure 2.4 Bilingualism in Ariaal and Rendille

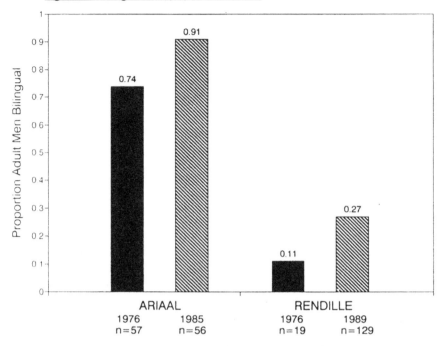

from towns, hospitals, and police protection. The desire for the *loibon's* protective medicines seemed a direct consequence of isolation and very real dangers of pastoral existence, particularly during periods of drought.[12]

Ariaal, Rendille and Samburu dress very similarly, and to a foreign observer are indistinguishable. All three societies have a visible warrior age grade, where initiated men between fifteen and thirty years old wear their hair in long, red-dyed braids, carry a variety of lethal weapons (spears, swords, and clubs), and wear ivory earrings. In contrast, women keep their hair closely shaven and wear extensive jewelry as beaded headbands, necklaces, and brass and aluminum bracelets and anklets. Elders, the least decorated group are easily distinguished by their shaven heads and long dangling earlobes and wear only simple sheets or blankets wrapped around their bodies.

Most Ariaal are bilingual in Samburu and Rendille; males in particular converse in Samburu. In 1976, 74% of adult Ariaal males were fully bilingual (compared to the monolingual Rendille of whom only 11% of the adult men could speak Samburu). By 1986 bilingualism had grown to 91% for Ariaal men and 27% for Rendille men (shown in Figure 2.4), mainly young elders who had entered the cattle economy, worked for wages, or gone to school.[13]

Age-Set Organization

Ariaal, like Samburu and Rendille, organize their society into age-grades
and age-sets. Age-grades are proscribed sets of behaviors and expectations
for members sharing the same stage in the life cycle, in Ariaal specifically
as boys, warriors, and elders for men, and as young girls, adolescent girls,
and circumcised (by clitoridectomy) married women for females. Each age-
grade has explicit rules about what clothes and ornaments they wear, what
foods they eat, or with whom they may associate. For example, adolescent
boys and married elders may milk camels, but warriors may not; warriors
may wear red, let their hair grow long and worn in red-dyed braids, but
boys may not. Warriors may not eat food prepared or seen by women, and
they prefer to live with other warriors "in the bush." Adolescent girls avoid
married men, including their own fathers. These ritualized prohibitions and
age-markers serve the function of segregating Ariaal society into specific
work groups, with warriors herding cattle in the distant camps, adolescent
boys responsible for camel herding, and adolescent girls herding small stock
close to the settlements. This division of labor is discussed in more detail
in the following chapter.

Men pass through the ladder of different age-grades as members of
specific age-sets, incorporated and named groups in which members remain
for life. Ariaal age-sets are initiated every fourteen years, where boys between
the ages of eleven and twenty five are circumcised with other members of
their clan. For the next fourteen years, members of the warrior set are
expected to herd animals in the distant camps and protect the settlements
from armed attack.

The age-set systems of the Ariaal and Rendille share similar features but
are two distinct institutions.[14] The Ariaal follow the Samburu, rather than
the Rendille, age-set ritual structure. Both Samburu and Ariaal perform
their circumcisions outside each settlement, and mark stages in their warriorhood by a series of five ritual ox-slaughters called *mugit*. The Rendille
do not have *mugit* rites, but have large clan based circumcision rituals
(*khandi*) followed by a single and inclusive ceremony called the *galgulumi*
in which the age-set is given its name.

Age-set affiliations cut across descent group relations and friendships are
formed for life between members of the same age-set. It is during their
period as warriors that men are socialized into adulthood, learn how to
manage livestock, and form contacts and friendships important to their
future grazing strategies.

Ariaal, like the Rendille and Samburu use their age-set names as historical
references to past events, and time and history are marked by references
to the age-sets. "When the *Tarigirik* (a named age-set) were warriors, we
took camels from the Laikipiak . . . ," meaning between the initiation of
the *Tarigirik* age-set (circa 1865) and the initiation of the *Marikon* set fourteen
years later (circa 1879), this event occurred. This system of named and
regular age-sets has enabled ethnohistorians to piece together the histories

Samburu warriors assemble for dance at a wedding, Barta plains

Table 2.1   Samburu, Ariaal, and Rendille Age-set Chronology

Age-sets and Initiation Year:

Samburu		Ariaal		Rendille	
Kipling	c.1837	Kipling	c. 1838	Ikubuku	c. 1839
Kiteku	c.1851	Kiteku	c. 1852	Libali	c. 1853
Tarigirik	c.1865	Tarigirik	c. 1866	Dibgudo	c. 1867
Merikon	c.1879	Merikon	c. 1881	Dismala	c. 1882
Terito	1893	Terito	1894	Irbangudo	1895
Merisho	1909	Merisho	1911	Difgudo	1912
Kiliako	1921	Kiliako	1923	Irbales	1923
Mekuri	1936	Mekuri	1937	Libale	1937
Kimaniki	1948	Kimaniki	1950	Irbandif	1951
Kishili	1962	Kishili	1964	Difgudo	1965
Kororo	1976	Kororo	1978	Irbangudo	1979
Maoli	1990	Maoli	1991/92		

(Source for Samburu and Rendille: Sobania 1980:135)

of many East African pastoralist groups. Table 2.1 lists the names of and dates for the initiation of warrior age-sets in Samburu, Ariaal, and Rendille.

Ariaal Settlements and
Descent Group Organization

Ariaal settlements are collections of families related by patrilineal descent, usually full and half brothers living together with their wives and children in individual households. Larger Ariaal settlements may include over twenty five males descended from a common patrilineal ancestor, and their families. Members of a clan settlement do not marry each other, as clans are usually exogamous, and the daughters of the clan settlement marry men in other clan settlements. About fifteen percent of Ariaal settlements are made up of non-agnatically related households, usually Rendille affines (in-laws) who have joined the Ariaal to seek their fortunes raising small stock and/or cattle.

Ariaal settlements are either lowland or highland communities, depending on whether they concentrate on raising camels and small stock (as Rendille) or cattle (as the Samburu). Highland settlements keep primarily cattle and are fairly permanent, living in well watered locations on Marsabit Mountain (at Karare or Logologo) or the Ndoto Mountains (at the headwaters of the Milgis and Merille Rivers). One of the most concentrated highland Ariaal communities is at Karare (also called Lorubai) on Marsabit Mountain, where over 1000 people, predominately from the Lorokush section, live in large and permanent settlements.

Lowland camel-keeping settlements are large and average twenty five houses (125 people). The settlement in which I lived, Lewogoso Lukumai, consisted of over fifty houses with 250 people in 1976. Keeping large herds of camels and small stock, Lewogoso stockowners also own many cattle which are managed for much of the year in herding camps in the Ndoto mountains. Like other Ariaal settlements, Lewogoso have strong ties with "brother" settlements practicing alternative economies, and there is a Lewogoso cattle-keeping settlement in the Mathews' Range Mountains to their south near Wamba. Those Ariaal keeping both camels and cattle will often live with their camels in the lowlands and herd their cattle in highland camps managed by the warriors and adolescents. The Ariaal live in over twenty five clan settlements, listed in Table 2.2. and shown on Map 2.2 shows the location of Ariaal settlements in relation to highland and lowland resources.

Ariaal settlements are organized by clan identity, and the Ariaal are incorporated in the Samburu (rather than the Rendille) segmentary descent group system. Samburu (and Ariaal) descent groups are organized within two moieties (the White Cattle and Black Cattle), each of which has four sections (called *marei*, the ribs). The four White Cattle sections are Lukumai, Lorokushu, Loimusi, and Longieli; the four Black Cattle sections are Masala, Pisikishu (Turia in Ariaal), Nyaparai (LeSarge in Ariaal), and Lng'wesi. Each

Map 2.2 Location of Ariaal Settlements

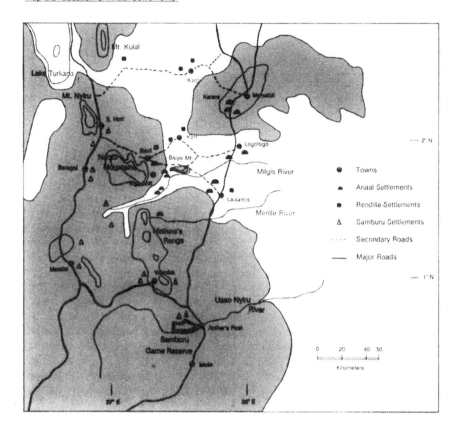

section is divided into clans (one to four in each section), which in turn are made up of sub-clans, lineages and sublineages. Settlements are usually local clans or sub-clans.

Ariaal political organization is based on their segmentary descent system; the closer the known agnatic (patrilineal) affiliation between descent groups, the greater their social solidarity in terms of economic exchanges, ritual inclusion, common residence, and political alliances. Conversely, the more distant the agnatic affiliation, the greater the competition between these groups for resources, marriage partners, and so on.

Segmentary systems characterize many "stateless" societies organized by lineal descent groups but lacking centralized political authority. In contrast to centralized chiefdoms (as traditional Somali or Zulu) or state-level kingdoms (as BaGanda or Ashanti), decisions and political processes in segmentary systems are made by collective discussions and consensus of all married men. (Women are usually excluded from major political discussions among the Ariaal.) Within each Ariaal local group, individual household heads are

Table 2.2 Distribution of Ariaal Settlements

Moiety	Section	Clan Settlement	Specialization	Location
White Cattle	Lukumai	Lewogoso	Camel	Ngurunit
		Lewogoso	Cattle	Milgis
		Mokadile	Camel	Laisamis
		Mokadile	Cattle	Milgis
		Soritari	Camel	Laisamis
		Soritari	Cattle	Logologo
		Parakeno	Cattle	Milgis
		Parakeno	Camels	Laisamis
	Longieli	Leparsinkir	Camels	Illaut
		Tarapasia	Cattle	Logologo
	Lorokushu	Pardopa	Camels	Laisamis
		Pardopa	Cattle	Marsabit
		Leparsile	Cattle	Logologo
		Makelelit	Camels	Laisamis
		Makelelit	Cattle	Marsabit
Black Cattle	Masala	Sortoi	Camels	Illaut
		Sortoi	Cattle	Ngurunit
		Kurtenkerta	Camels	Laisamis
		Kurtenkerta	Cattle	Ngurunit
	LeSarge	Goborre	Camels	Korr
	Turia	Ferlach	Camels	Laisamis
	(Pisikishu)	Ferlach	Cattle	Marsabit
		Dohole	Camels	Laisamis
		Marlene	Cattle	Milgis
		Gobonai	Camels	Laisamis

free to move where they please (or are able), and conflicts may be resolved by fissioning of the local group when two protagonists simply separate. More often however, the collective group of elders will appeal to the solidarity of the kinship group and attempt (usually successfully) to resolve conflicts and restore peaceful relations between brothers, settlements, lineage, and clans.

Segmentary descent organization among Ariaal and Rendille appears to be an adaptation to an environment of high variability, rather than to warfare or "predatory expansion" as argued for groups like the Nuer of Sudan.[15] Ariaal domestic settlements periodically fission and fuse depending on environmental conditions and the type of livestock resources a household owns. Those with predominately cattle herds will move closer to the mountains and permanent water in the dry seasons, while those with large camel herds will move some distance from crowded and overgrazed water holes using pack camels to haul water for the human group. Settlements

Adolescent girl applying makeup to her sister

will also fission based on social conflicts and contracts, where several households move to more favorable grazing areas based on ties of marriages, while others may separate based on inter-family tensions and animosities.

Summary

Ariaal are a community of camel, cattle, and small stock pastoralists who emerged as a social formation in northern Kenya during the disastrous period of the late 19th century.

Related to both the Rendille and the Samburu, Ariaal are ambivalent about their social identity. Distinct from Rendille, Ariaal see themselves (and are seen by others) as people who keep cattle as well as camels and small stock, speak both Rendille and Samburu, and follow both Rendille and Samburu customs. Ariaal view Rendille and Samburu as important allies against common enemies (particularly Turkana and Boran) and as a channel for their own pastoral movements.

One might argue, as Barth does, that cultural identity is forged in the process of particular adaptations to particular "ecological niches."[16] Certainly Ariaal have adopted those features of Rendille culture consistent with camel production, and those features of Samburu conducive to cattle production. But Ariaal identity is not simply a question of ecological adaptation, it is a consequence of specific historical and social processes. Turkana pastoralists to the west of Lake Turkana occupy a similar environment to the Ariaal—arid, topographically diverse, and isolated—and Turkana too have a tripartite pastoral system keeping cattle, camels and small stock. Yet Turkana live in small and isolated household groupings rather than the large clan settlements of Ariaal and Rendille. The differences between these pastoralist groups are social and historical, and while ecological factors act as constraints on human organization, they do not determine what social forms society follows.

Ariaal identity is ambiguous because ethnic identity is in itself ambiguous. Restricted by "tribal boundaries" imposed by the colonial government, Ariaal may "choose" affiliation with Rendille in order to remain in Marsabit District, while at another time claim Samburu identity, such as in schools or the army.[17] In fact, ethnic identity or affiliation may reflect more the European need to categorize rather than reflect actual boundaries and divisions between groups themselves.

Ariaal do exist "on the ground," even if they do not fit neatly in an ethnographic atlas. We now turn our attention to how Ariaal organize their pastoral production, and to the dialectic tension between cooperation and competition between individual households for grazing resources.

Notes

1. Sperling 1987a.

2. See Spear 1981 for an introduction to the pre-colonial history of Kenya. For detailed archaeological evidence see Ambrose 1982; Phillipson 1988; for linguistic history of Nilotes and Cushites see Ehret 1971, 1974, 1984; Heine 1979; Heine et al. 1979; Vossen 1978, 1982.

3. For ethnohistory of Maasai, see Berntsen 1976, 1979; Jacobs 1965; Waller 1978, 1985, 1988; for pastoralists in northern Kenya see Lamphear 1976, 1988; Sobania 1980a, 1988, [In Press]; Spencer 1973.

4. Spencer 1973:153–154; Sobania [In Press].

5. Sobania 1980a:137; Waller 1988:75–77.

6. Chanler 1896:292–93, 306–313.

7. Interview with Kawap Bulyar, Korr, Oct. 18 1985.

8. Sobania 1980a:191–2.

9. Fratkin [In Press].

10. Interview with KiToip Lenkiribe, Ngurunit, Oct. 24, 1985.

11. For a discussion of Rendille and Samburu ritual, see Spencer 1973.

12. Fratkin 1991.

13. Fratkin [In Press]. Heine (1976) found that Ariaal men were more likely to speak Samburu as women.

14. See Beaman 1981, Fleming 1965, Fratkin 1987b, and Spencer 1965, 1973 for discussion of Samburu and Rendille age-set systems.

15. Segmentary descent systems were initially described by Evans-Pritchard (1940:6) for the Nuer of Sudan as an acephalous and often factional collection of related but autonomous descent groups composed of patrilineally related individuals. Sahlins

(1961) argued that the system served for expansion by warfare of Nuer groups, and Kelly (1985) argued that segmentary expansion enabled accumulation of cattle for bridewealth.

16. Barth 1956.

17. Fratkin [In Press].

Livestock Production and Human Nutrition

3 Ariaal live in a semi-desert environment of very sparse resources. Low and variable rainfall, marked seasonality in vegetation growth, and few watering areas make Marsabit District too dry to support agriculture on a wide scale, and nearly all the area's residents depend on domestic livestock to survive. From the perspective of human ecology, pastoralists use their domestic animals to convert patchy and seasonal vegetative resources into a constant supply of food in the form of milk, meat, blood, and a surplus with which to trade for grains, tea and sugar.

Despite its aridity, the semi-desert of northern Kenya supports sizable herds of animals, both wild and domestic. Grazing side by side with Ariaal cattle, camels, goats and sheep are giraffe, Grant's gazelles, gerenuks (desert antelopes with long graceful necks), and even elephants. There are also the predators of these herbivores, particularly lion and hyena, and to a lesser extent cheetah, leopard, and wild dog.

The essential strategy of livestock pastoralism is to ensure adequate grazing and water for their livestock to provide a regular and food supply for the human community. Herders follow certain practices aimed at keeping their herds productive through both seasonal variations as well as extensive periods of drought. These practices are principally herd diversification and herd mobility.

Herd diversity enables a pastoralist to utilize different micro environments as well as providing insurance against particular herd loss, such as cattle to pneumonia or camels to glanders disease. In 1984 when Samburu and Ariaal lost over half their cattle to drought, Ariaal were able to rely on their camels who were relatively unscathed. Furthermore, the keeping of different types of animals offers complementary food resources as well as different breeding and milking cycles. Ariaal rely on their camels for milk and transport, their small stock of goats and sheep for meat and trade, and their cattle to provide both traditional exchange values (bridewealth and ritual slaughters) as well as trade in the commercial market for cash.

Of equal if not greater importance than herd diversity in arid environments is mobility. Because of the high seasonality in rainfall and the high evaporation rate, vegetation resources deteriorate very quickly. Herds are taken to new

Tapping blood from a goat, Lewogoso settlement

green pastures following isolated rain fall, as pastures are more nutritive during growing season, with higher proportions of crude protein and carbohydrates. These movements are limited mainly by the availability of drinking water, which although widespread in the wet seasons, is found only in a few areas with permanent water holes during the dry season. The responsibility of feeding their animals is perhaps the single greatest factor affecting Ariaal settlement and labor organization.

Each type of stock has its own particular feeding requirements and grazing environment. Cattle are grazers (grass-eaters) who need water every two to three days, and consequently must be herded in the wetter highlands. Camels are adapted to desert conditions, preferring browse (stems and leaves) of shrubs and trees that thrive when grasses are desiccated. Furthermore, camels can go without watering for ten days, offering enough time for their herders to graze them extensively in the desert lowlands between fixed water points. Small stock can thrive in the deserts, but like cattle need water every two to three days, and must be grazed near the mountain springs and wells.

Because of these different herding requirements, Ariaal separate their animals into domestic herds (milk camels, small stock for meat, and male camels and donkeys for transport) and camp (*fora*) herds (mainly non-milking stock) which are herded in distant grazing areas. Ariaal settlements are semi-sedentary and situated near permanent water sources and small urban centers with shops. People do not generally live closer than ten kilometers to the waterholes, as they would overgraze the available vegetation quickly and have to graze their animals at greater distances. The chance of finding better pastures increases with the distance from the water points.

The Semi-Desert Environment

Ariaal settlements are clustered near permanent water along the base of the Ndoto Mountains and Mt. Marsabit, yet due to their ties to Samburu and Rendille, Ariaal have access to a herding environment of approximately 10,000 square kilometers. This area is topographically diverse, ranging from lowland desert over much of the area to highland grazing in the Ndotos, Marsabit Mountain, and Mt. Kulal. Most of this grazing area is too dry to use except briefly in the rainy periods, particularly the Chalbi and Kaisut Deserts; other areas are restricted or inaccessible, such as the forested reserve on Marsabit Mountain which is prohibited to pastoralists except during the severest droughts. For the most part, Ariaal confine their herding of cattle to highland river valleys along the Milgis River or the drier forests of Mt. Marsabit, their camels in Rendille lowlands of the Kaisut Desert, and their small stock close to the permanent settlements along the valley river beds.

Rainfall and Water Resources

Marsabit District is the most arid region in Kenya, receiving an average of 500mm of rainfall each year. Where rainfall on Mt. Marsabit or Mt. Kulal (at Gatab) may exceed 1000mm annually, rainfall in the Kaisut and Chalbi Desert (at Oltorot) may be less than 200mm a year, as shown in Figure 3.1. The rainfall is erratic and irregular in quantity and timing, and no one can predict where, when, or how much rain will fall with any degree of accuracy. Figure 3.2 shows yearly rainfall variability on Marsabit Mountain between 1919 and 1982. Temperatures are more constant with a mean of 27.8°C. in the lowlands and 18.9°C. in the highlands, with little monthly or seasonal differences.[1]

When rainfall occurs, it tends to be concentrated in two seasons, a long rain (*lng'erng'erwa* in Samburu, *Guu* in Rendille) between March and May, and a short rain (*tumerin* in Samburu, *yer* in Rendille) in October and November. The period between November and March is called "the long hunger" (*lamai lo'odo* in Samburu, *nabhaider* in Rendille), and between June and October the "short hunger" (*lamai dorrop* in Samburu, *nahaigaban* in Rendille). This rainfall pattern conforms to the Inter-Tropical Convergence Zone (ITCZ) schedule when dry, high-pressure northeast trade winds from Arabia move southwest in the winter, and moist low-pressure Southeast trade winds flow northwest from the Indian Ocean in the summer.

Rainfall is critical to Ariaal pastoral economy for two major reasons: it directly determines vegetation growth and the availability of pasture for the livestock; and it provides drinking water for the human and livestock populations.

Figure 3.1 Monthly Rainfall in Marsabit District

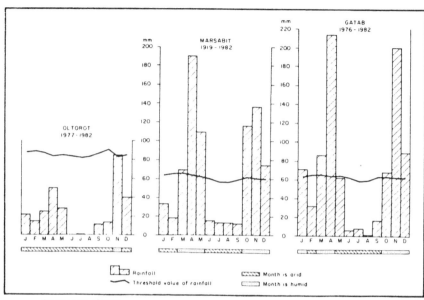

Source: IPAL 1984:51

Figure 3.2 Variability of Annual Rainfall in Marsabit District

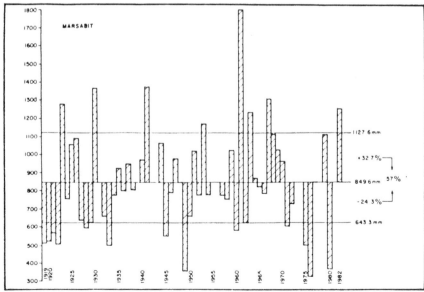

Source: IPAL 1984: 38

Map 3.1 Ariaal Water and Grazing Resources

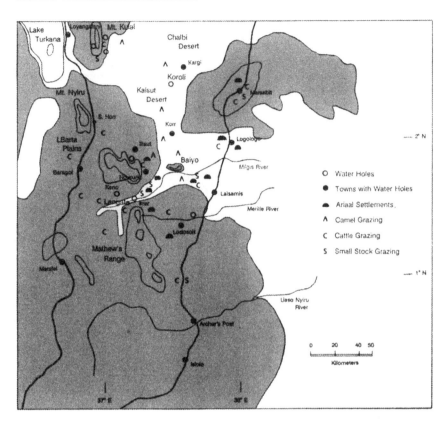

During wet periods, Ariaal have sufficient use of surface water in rain pools, semi-permanent rivers, and temporary flood plains, the most important surface water being the river runoffs from the Ndoto and Mathews Range mountains along the Ngurunit, Milgis, Merille, and Uaso Nyiru rivers. These rivers are sand-bedded, and the water quickly goes underground close to the mountain base. The Milgis River becomes a seasonal swamp to the west of Baiyo Mountain at Larapasie and is an important wet season watering point for Ariaal cattle and small stock. Map 3.1 shows Ariaal water and grazing resources.

In dry seasons, Ariaal must seek water in hand dug wells, which are located at points where non-porous rock trap laterally flowing water from the mountain runoffs. The locations of these trapped ground waters have been known to pastoralists through generations of trial and error digging. Wells traditionally are dug by hand, but many have been mechanized as boreholes in the past twenty years, particularly at Laisamis, Logologo, Halisuruwa (Korr), and Koroli near the Kargi settlement in Rendille. These permanent waterholes were developed by Christian missions, which have attracted permanent settlement by Rendille and Ariaal.

In general, camels prefer saline water found in the desert wells at Korr or Kargi, while cattle and small stock utilize the run-off and surface water in the mountains. This pattern may vary particularly as domestic milk camels are watered close to the Ariaal settlements at Ngurunit and Illaut, and cattle and small stock owned by Rendille may drink from the wells at Korr and Laisamis during periods when there is temporary grazing in the lowlands.

Vegetation

Vegetation in Marsabit District falls within four ecological zones:

1) highland forests above 2000 meters consisting of evergreen forests (*Juniper, Olea, Croton,* and *Strychnos* trees), constituting 5% of the Ariaal proper grazing area;
2) savanna-woodlands at 1000–1400 meters characterized by *Acacia nilotica* and *combretum* trees with a dense grass cover (*themeda, digitaria,* and *chrysopogon*). This ecological zone is found on Mt. Marsabit and the Ndoto Mountains, and although making up less than 10% of the Ariaal grazing environment, it is the area most exploited by Ariaal cattle, particularly in the foothills of the Ndoto Mountains;
3) arid scrub bushland between 700 and 1000 meters, representing about 30% of Ariaal resources. This dry sandy semi-desert of mixed *acacia-commiphora* trees (particularly *Acacia tortillis* and *Acacia senegal*) and perennial grasses (*leptochloa* and *enteropogon*) offers the main dry season grazing for Ariaal camels and location for Ariaal settlements subsisting off domestic stock of milk-camels;
4) very arid desert comprising 55% of the Ariaal area (the Kaisut Desert) at an altitude of 200–800 meters and receiving annual rainfall less than 200mm. Despite its extreme aridity, periodic rains will produce a large but short-lived growth of annual grasses and shrubs (*aristida, tetrapogon, tephrosia,* and *portulaca*) which are eaten by camels and small stock in the short wet seasons.

Ariaal also utilize two micro-environments in the area—lava plateaux (called *marti*), 700–1000 meters high and found throughout the arid semi-desert which provide shrubs and tall perennial grasses exploited by camels and small stock in the dry season; and riverine woodlands formed along river beds (composed of *ficus,* doum palm (*hyphaenae*), *salvadora,* and *lawsonia* trees, many of which are used in the manufacture of household goods). Ariaal settlements are often located close to these river beds, providing shade for the human community and food resources for the domestic flocks of small stock.[2]

Table 3.1. Livestock Holdings per capita in Ariaal and Rendille

	Human Pop.	Camel	Cattle	Goats	Sheep
Ariaal (1976)	269	1.6	4.6	5.2	2.7
Ariaal (1985)	239	2.7	3.6	8.8	4.4
Rendille (1976--81) (aerial survey)	12,900	1.4	1.9	5.0	3.3

Source: Fratkin 1987a; IPAL 1984:286

Ariaal Livestock

Ariaal own large numbers of livestock, averaging 1–3 camels, 3–5 cattle, and 8–13 small stock per person. These numbers are similar to the Rendille, but Ariaal have larger cattle herds and smaller camel holdings. Table 3.1 shows gives comparative livestock holdings of Ariaal and Rendille.

Despite the large sizes of both Rendille and Ariaal herds, these livestock are highly variable in productivity (milk and meat offtake and reproductive growth). They reproduce in low numbers and suffer high mortalities due to high rates of disease, infertility, malnutrition, and parasite loads, particularly during and immediately after extensive droughts. Ariaal lost over 50% of their cattle in the 1982–1984 drought, primarily to starvation and pneumonia, while their camels, suffering less from drought, nevertheless typically lose 30% of their infants from diseases including trypanosomiasis and tick toxicity. Goats and sheep also succumbed to pneumonia as well as brucellosis and all stock types have very large loads of intestinal worms.[3] McCabe's study of four Turkana households through the drought of 1980 recorded mortalities of 55% of their cattle herds (65% directly to bovine pneumonia); 45% of their camels (33% starved, 25% died of disease, and 39% were stolen or predated); and 48% of their goats and 76% of their sheep, due to starvation, disease, and heat stress.[4]

The Ariaal strategy for coping with these hazards is to keep large numbers of different food-producing stock (cattle, camels, goats and sheep), maximize their herd sizes as insurance against catastrophic loss, and disperse their animals by herding their livestock in separate areas and loaning their animals to friends and kin in distant areas.

Ariaal depend on their livestock primarily for milk, which constitutes 70% of the diet in the pastoral settlements, complemented by meat, store-bought grains, sugar and tea, and occasionally blood tapped from living animals. The majority of the Ariaal herds are female (estimated at 55% of the cattle, 60–70% of the camels, and 50–60% of their small stock) with a high proportion of mature adults so that 15–25% of their livestock are in milk at any given time. Males are kept primarily for meat and exchange, and are all castrated with the exception of one to two bulls and rams.[5]

The milk and meat yields and growth rates of different Ariaal livestock are described in Table 3.2, compiled from ecological studies of Boran, Turkana, and Rendille pastoralists.

Table 3.2 Production Characteristics of East African Livestock

	Camels	Cattle	Goats	Sheep
Mean weight	300kg	164.7	24.8	23.7
Daily Milk yields for human consumption (liters)				
Wet season	2.5	1.3	.23	.22
Dry season	1.2	0.5	.09	.07
Lactation length (months)	12	6.9	4.6	4.5
Herd growth rate (%)	1.5	2.5	11	11
Birthing interval (months)	24	18	5.5	8.3

Source: Dahl and Hjort (1976), IPAL (1984), and Dyson-Hudson (1982).

Camels

Camels are Ariaal's largest milk producers, yielding an average of 3.5–4.0 liters daily of which 2.2 liters are available for human consumption. Furthermore, the supply of camel milk is lengthy and copious. Lactation lasts from 9–18 months and does not end during the dry season as it may with cattle or small stock.

Camels are remarkable animals with an unusual ability to thrive in deserts, areas characterized by high temperatures, lack of water, and plant life too saline for other ruminants. They can go without watering almost two weeks, and are watered by Ariaal and Rendille every ten days, allowing them, to be grazed over a wide area. The adaptations of camels to arid regions are based on their efficiency to utilize available moisture and their economical expenditure of body fluids, including very dry feces and highly concentrated urine. (Like birds but unlike other mammals, camels excrete uric acid rather than urea).[6]

Despite their adaptation to arid lands, camels have a very low growth rate of 1.5% annually due to both a low birth rate and a high mortality rate. A camel dam drops her first calf in her sixth year, following a long gestation period of 12–13 months. A long lactation period averaging 12 months contributes to a 26–30 month birth interval. Furthermore, between 30–60% of Ariaal calves less than one year old died in untreated herds, primarily because of trypanosomes (blood parasites) and toxins produced by heavy tick infestations. The avoidance of these insects is a major reason Ariaal settlements are located away from mountain locations with their greater density of vegetation and arthropod vectors of disease. Other diseases found in camel populations include viral infections (rinderpest, foot and mouth disease, rabies), bacteria (tuberculosis, salmonellosis, contagious pleuropneumonia, glanders), larger internal parasites (trypanosomiasis, coccidiosis, leishmaniasis, arterial filariasis), and external parasites (mange, ticks). Studies by IPAL veterinary scientists suggest that adequate veterinary care could improve camel productivity in Rendille by 100%.[7]

In addition to milk production, camels are the main pack animal of Ariaal. Male animals transport houses and household goods during settlement relocations, and fetch water for human consumption. Married women are responsible for loading and working the transport camels, and will collect water for the household every third or fourth day, labor that usually requires a walk of 10–15 kilometers.

Cattle

Like Samburu, Ariaal keep the Borana breed of East African Zebu cattle, which are characterized by a back hump (used like the camel to store fat, providing calories in drought conditions), short horns, and loose skinfold (dewlap) under the neck (a cooling adaptation). Hair colors vary—white, red, black, and mottled—but white predominates in the lowland herds. Borana cattle have a hardy reputation for surviving in dry and marginal rangeland, eating grasses when possible, but subsisting on browse if necessary.

Ariaal cattle cannot survive in the dry lowlands to which camels are so well suited because of their need for free water at least once every three days (and preferably every other day). In addition, cattle must be taken to natural salt licks found along river beds. Cattle can also tolerate higher tick loads than camels (tse-tse flies are not found in Marsabit District) and so are herded primarily in the forested highlands.

Cattle produce much less milk than camels, slightly more than 1.0 liter in wet periods and as little as 250cc in the dry season, and one camel in year-round lactation can support as many people as four cows. Cattle lactate for a period of 3 to 8 months annually (with about 60% of the herd being female and 50% per year) and can provide between 0.5 and 1.5 liters for human consumption daily.[8]

Although their milk production is low, cattle have a high reproductive rate, twice that of camels, with 9 months gestation, 8 months lactation, and a year-round mating period. A cow can be expected to reproduce after 17 months while a camel has a birth interval of 24 months.

This high birth rate produces a surplus of large animals that contributes to their use for trade and rituals. Eight cattle are the ideal Samburu and Ariaal bridewealth, and steers are ritually slaughtered at weddings and age-set ceremonies. A main economic role of cattle in Ariaal is as a traditional exchange medium for wives, and Ariaal and increasingly Rendille will try to build up their cattle herds to gain additional wives in polygyny. Cattle are also increasingly becoming the main source of cash income for Ariaal, providing more than half of their cash needs through trade and livestock auctions.

As shown in Table 3.3, cattle provided over 75% of Lewogoso's cash income in both 1976 and 1985. Ariaal households sold a significantly larger proportion of their small stock in 1976 as in 1985, as they preferred to build up their small stock flocks following the widespread loss of cattle during the 1984 drought. Interestingly, the Ariaal also loaned and begged small stock to a higher degree in 1985 than 1976, showing the importance of gift giving and maintaining social ties in periods of hardship.

Ariaal stockowners prefer to sell cattle rather than camels because of their high growth rate, the relatively high prices cattle fetch on the market, and their lower milk yields.

Table 3.3 Use of Livestock in Lewogoso Exchanges, 1976[a] and 1985[b]

	CAMELS		CATTLE		SMALL STOCK	
	1976	1985	1976	1985	1976	1985
No. Owned/household	18	20	41	26	89	108
No. Sold	0	0	4.6	2.0	12.2	4.9
No. Loaned	0.4	0.9	0.56	0.4	0.9	2.3
No. Begged	0.36	0.12	0.23	0.3	.96	1.4
Cash Value (K.Sh.)	1500	4000	250	1085	25	150
Total Cash Income (K.Sh.)	0	0	1150	2170	305	735
Total Cash Income ($US)[c]	0	0	138.5	135.6	36.7	45.9

a. 1976: 30 households, pop. 236.
b. 1985: 32 households, pop. 258.
c. 1976 $1.00 = 8.3 Kenyan shillings; 1985 $1.00 = 16.0 K. Sh.

The role of cattle as a cash provider is particularly important to Ariaal who depend on store-bought maizemeal to supplement or substitute for milk during the dry seasons. The average Ariaal household in Lewogoso settlement in 1976 spent 360 Kenyan shillings ($38.00) for maizemeal; in 1985 that figure had doubled to 1200 shillings ($75.00 adjusted for inflation). Grain purchases were substantially higher in the settled towns like Korr where Rendille families, largely without stock, were buying maizemeal (*posho*) daily, spending over 1500 shillings a year and receiving from the mission free posho and powdered milk during drought or other hardship conditions.

Small Stock

Ariaal keep large numbers of small stock, averaging sixty goats and sheep per household; some household flocks are over 300. Small stock are an important part of Ariaal pastoral economy because of their high reproductive rate, their ability to survive in arid conditions, their easy convertibility to cash, and because they provide a ready source of meat.

Ariaal and Rendille keep goats of the Small East African type, and sheep of the short-haired Somali (Persian) breed, weighing about 20 kilograms each. Ariaal have more goats than a ratio of about 2:1, a fact attributed to the goats better adaptability to arid environments.[9]

Sheep and goats are herded together and called by a collective name [*ntare* for mixed flocks; *lkine* (*lkineji* pl.) for goats and *nker* (*nkerra* pl.) for sheep, Samburu]. Like camels, small stock prefer to graze in the hot tickless plains where goats prefer browse (twigs and leaves) and sheep prefer grasses. Their mutually high water needs, however, demand that small stock are grazed near permanent water sources, usually close to the mountain foothills. For much of the year, small stock remain with the domestic settlements; only in very dry situations are they grazed in camps. Small stock are difficult to herd—individuals can wander off and they easily develop infections from thorns or stones between the hooves, particularly in wet conditions.

Goats and sheep are poor milk producers. During a 3 month lactation period a goat can be expected to provide 200cc of milk daily in wet periods, and as little as 50cc in the dry periods; hence 20 goats are necessary to provide 1 liter of milk in the dry months. Their primary importance lies in their high reproductive rates due to a short birth interval, short gestation period, a high number of twin births. Poor milk producers, goats and sheep are used mainly for meat and exchange. Ariaal also concentrate on building up their small stock following a drought, for they recover quickly and can be traded for cash or directly for large livestock, particularly cattle. An Ariaal stockowner explained, "Small stock are our bank. When we need cash or something to settle a dispute, we have our goats and sheep."

Small stock are killed with increasing frequency as the dry season progresses, and it is not unusual for a household to butcher a goat or sheep each week. In addition to consuming the meat, hides are made into women's skirts or sold to traders for small amounts (25 Kenyan shillings or US$ 2.00). Most importantly, small stock are sold at local shops for about 150 K. sh. each (US$ 6.25) and contribute up to 40% of a household's cash needs.

Miscellaneous Animals

Ariaal also keep donkeys and dogs, neither of which are used for food. Donkeys are kept as pack animals by some Ariaal, particularly those in the highlands owing to the donkey's high water and grazing needs. They are not found widely among lowland Ariaal who use male camels for transporting water and household goods.

Dogs are kept by Ariaal and Rendille to warn against predators. Unlike Turkana who allow their dogs to lick the feces from their babies,[10] Ariaal do not allow the dogs to touch or come too close to humans. Over half of Lewogoso households had at least one dog, short-haired, red-and-white or black-and-white basenji-type animals (although they bark, unlike basenjis). Dogs are fed scraps, but must obtain their water when domestic herds are watered. Ariaal confess that their dogs are treated worse than any other type of livestock they own.

The Division of Camp and Settlement

Ariaal separate their livestock into domestic settlement herds of milking stock, loading animals, and juvenile or nursing stock, and mobile camp herds for non-lactating and non-transport animals. The mobile camps (called *fora* in Rendille and Ariaal and *lalei* in Samburu) graze the surplus animals in their particular grazing areas, managed by a specific section of the labor force—the cattle in highland camps managed by warriors, camels in the lowland tended mainly by adolescent boys, and small stock herded near the domestic settlements by adolescent boys and girls.[11]

During the dry season, which may last 9–12 months per year, Ariaal cattle are taken into highland locations such as Irrer and Langata on the

Milgis River, returning home to the settlements only during brief rains when there is sufficient grazing in the lowlands. Camels are grazed in the northern deserts near Rendille camps for much of the dry season, but if there is sufficient water they will stay with Ariaal settlements. The bulk of the small stock remain with the settlements, joining the cattle camps only in drought conditions when the grazing is too poor.

The settlement will keep nearly all milking camels, nursing young and those male camels used for transport. Within the settlement reside married adults, adolescent girls and boys, and young children. Adolescent boys graze the camels, adolescent girls manage the loading camels to fetch water, and younger children graze small stock and fetch firewood. It is essential that the settlement has access to adequate grazing and water for the domestic stock.

Herding Routine of Lewogoso
Lukumai Settlement, 1975–1976

Lewogoso residents claim the area along the Ndoto Mountains near Lependera Rock, between Ngurunit and Baiyo Mountain, as their traditional home, and prefer to remain in that location as long as pasture, water, and security is adequate. Lewogoso settlement remained at Lependera until April 1975, when heavy rains made the Larapasie swamp west of Baiyo Mountain attractive for domestic livestock, particularly cattle and small stock. The settlement moved about 10 km southeast from Lependera, about 8 km directly west of the swamp. Lewogoso remained in the Larapasie area for 18 months, shifting locations 2 km west in June 1976 after a death in the settlement. (See Map 3.1)

During 1974–1976, Lewogoso cattle spent very little time near the settlement, returning from distant grazing only during of June 1974, the spring rains of 1975, and the October rains of 1976. For the most part, the cattle grazed in the highland valleys of Langata, about 60 km to the southeast in the Ndotos along the Milgis River. Some cattle grazed in Samburu District 100 km to the northwest in the Barta plains, as this area experienced good rains in October 1975 and again in April 1976, when the rains failed on the eastern side.

While the cattle were grazing in highland locations, Lewogoso's camels were herded quite close to the settlement, often returning at night from grazing on the *marti* plateaux south of Baiyo mountain, watering at either the Ngurunit or Irrer water holes. Brief rains in October 1975 enabled the camel camps to shift to the salt-rich browse and water near Korr in central Rendille, 40 km east. However, when the drought intensified with the failure of the spring rains in 1976 (and the drying up of the Ngurunit wells), the camels were taken north and west 60km to Mount Kulal and Mount Nyiru, where they remained until October 1976 when the fall rains enabled them to return to the Irrer area and the domestic settlement.

Lewogoso small stock not remaining in the settlement followed the cattle herding routine during 1974–1976, grazing for much of the time at the

Warriors repair well at cattle camp, Marsabit Mountain

Langata-Keno pastures along the Milgis River, although some flocks followed those cattle camps that grazed in the Barta plains in April 1976. Both flocks returned to the Ngurunit-Larapasie area in October 1976 during the fall rains.

When I returned ten years later in 1985, these grazing areas had not altered, except that neither Ariaal nor Rendille were herding any stock near the Turkana at Barta plains or near Mt. Kulal due to increasing encroachment by Turkana settlements and herds in those areas. In the dry period between October 1985 and March 1986, Lewogoso's cattle were grazed in traditional highland locations such as Irrer and Keno, while the small stock stayed closer to the domestic settlement in the area of the Larapasie, which, though dried into a flat pan, still had sufficient water in the hand-dug wells. Many of Lewogoso's camels were kept in the settlement during this period, because there was adequate watering and pasture in the Ngurunit area, but some camels herds were taken closer to the wells at Korr and Koroli (near Kargi).

The Division of Labor in Livestock Tasks

Production tasks in Ariaal Rendille are performed by different social categories based on age and gender roles in the division of labor. Adolescent boys and warriors perform most of the camel and cattle herding tasks;

Figure 3.3 Daytime Activities by Gender and Age, Lewogoso Settlement

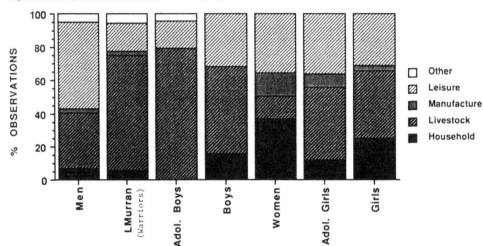

adolescent girls and small boys herd the domestic small stock near the
settlement; adolescent girls fetch water from the wells utilizing pack camels;
and young girls assist in child-care and fetch firewood. Married women
milk the domestic settlement's cattle and small stock, maintain houses, and
provide child-care and veterinary care to nursing stock. Married men, or
elders, are responsible for animal husbandry (selecting bulls), milking camels,
tracking lost animals, providing veterinary care, digging and maintaining
wells, and undertaking ritual and political leadership for the settlement.

The following figure shows the distribution of tasks of age and gender
categories in Lewogoso based on time-allocation surveys performed in
October 1985 and January 1986. These figures show the percentage of time
(based on the number of observations) each age and gender group was
seen performing specific tasks of housework (cooking, child care, cleaning),
livestock (grazing, watering, veterinary care, marketing), manufacturing
(household goods, leather, wood, rope, house construction), and leisure time
(resting, chatting, playing, singing).[12]

As reflected in Figure 3.3, woman spent 36.7% of their day in household
tasks while married men spent only 7.2% in household (a category which
included "eating"!). Whereas adult men spent 33% of their time in livestock
tasks, women spent 14% of their day with animals, mainly in milking but
also in herding and some veterinary care. Adolescent boys and warriors
spent the most time in livestock tasks (83% and 71% of their daytime
respectively), while adolescent girls also spent a considerable time in herding
and livestock activities (44%). Married men had the most leisure time
(52.4%) compared to 35% for married women and only 17% for adolescents
and warriors.

Much of Ariaal's daily labor is expended managing their herds. The care
of livestock never stops; they require attention from sunrise to late evening,

Table 3.4 Herding Labor Force by Location, Lewogoso Lukumai Settlement, October 21, 1985

	Settlement Herd			Fora Herd			Total
	camel	cattle	ss	camel	cattle	ss	
Married Men (>35)	0	1	3	0	0	1	5
Married Women (>22)	0	0	2	0	0	1	3
Warriors (22--34)	1	3	2	0	13	6	25
Males (12--21)	6	2	1	0	3	7	19
Females (12--21)	0	2	3	0	0	6	11
Boys (6--11)	9	1	0	0	0	0	10
Girls (6-11)	0	2	10	0	0	0	12

requiring adequate grazing, water and salt, and human protection to survive. Even at night when the animals are put into their enclosures, hungry predators or human enemies may attack.

The majority of actual herding is accomplished by adolescents and young adults. Table 3.4 describes the location and composition of livestock herders from Lewogoso Lukumai settlement during one day's herding in October 1985. This was a transitional period with slight rainfall, when all the camels were in settlement, but the bulk of the cattle and small stock herds were in *fora* camps.

Camels are herded exclusively by men and boys. Boys between six and eleven years watch over juvenile and infant camels grazing from the settlement. Older adolescents and a few members of the warrior age-set accompany non-milking adult camels to *fora* camps and watering locations. Young boys may begin to accompany animals to *fora* by the time they are eight or nine years old.

Cattle are herded for much of the year in mountain camps managed predominately by members of the warrior age set but also by adolescent boys and girls. Girls are principally responsible for managing the small stock flocks which are usually herded from the domestic settlements close to the permanent water sources. Although there is a sexual division of labor in livestock tasks, it is apparent that unmarried girls play a significant role in livestock production, particularly in daily herding tasks.

Livestock Production and Human Nutrition

Ariaal production of camels, cattle, and small stock provide three types of foods consumed by Ariaal—milk, meat, and blood. These foods provide about 75% of their daily calories and 90% of daily protein during the wet season, and about 60% in the dry season. Grains, tea and sugar are increasingly consumed as milk supplies diminish during the dry season, and are paid for by the sale of skins and livestock, particularly cattle and goats. Cash income is also used to buy cloth, rubber sandals, cooking utensils, and beads for jewelry.

Milk is the main food in Ariaal, as it is for other East African pastoralists.[13] Milk is consumed daily by all members of the society, either fresh following the morning and evening milking, or curdled ("the milk that sleeps" *nkule na oto*), which is consumed mainly by older males.

Camels are the most important milk producers in Ariaal settlements, providing an average of 0.8 liters milk per person per day.[14] Cattle produce an average of 1.0 liters of milk each daily, ranging from 0.5 to 1.5 liters depending on the condition of pasture and length of lactation. However, because cattle are herded away from the lowland Ariaal settlements for much of the year, they play only a minor role in settlement subsistence and mainly feed their camp herders. During wet seasons, cattle will return to the domestic settlements and contribute to the milk supply. During good periods of rainfall, cattle produce enough milk fat to make butter. Ariaal do not make cheese products.

With average household herds of 3–4 milk camels; 3–4 milk cows, and 9–12 milk goats and sheep, Ariaal have access to an average of 1.5 liters of milk per person daily. However, actual milk consumption varies by both seasonal supplies and by differential consumption patterns based on age, gender, and wealth differences. A warrior in a cattle camp may drink 2–3 liters of milk mixed with blood, while settlement children may have access only to 1.0 liter or less of milk daily. In the dry season when milk yields are reduced, households which own only a few camels may have no milk and depend on store-bought grains to survive. The grains, usually maizemeal and sometimes wheat flour, are made as porridge, consumed with milk, sugar, and butter in good times, or just plain in bad times.

Maasai and other pastoralists are renowned for drinking blood tapped from living animals. In Ariaal it is mainly warriors in livestock camps who consume blood, which is taken whole or, more often, mixed with milk. Women will eat cooked blood obtained from slaughtered animals, but avoid fresh blood as "too strong" except at childbirth when they are given blood "to gain strength." Blood is obtained from a living animal, usually gelded males of both large and small stock, by puncturing the jugular vein (or facial vein in a camel) with a small bow and specialized "blood" arrow. The vein of the animal, revealed by constricting the neck with a leather thong, is punctured by the arrow which bounces out immediately from the pressure of the gushing stream of blood. The blood is collected in small woven container, usually four liters from a camel or an ox, and one liter from a small stock. When the bleeding is completed, the leather tie is loosened and the bleeding stops. Stock are not bled more than once every three or four weeks each, yet it is estimated that a male camel will provide 35 liters of blood for human consumption annually.[15]

As the dry season progresses and milk resources are depleted, meat and maizemeal are increasingly consumed as households slaughter or sell goats, sheep, and to a lesser extent cattle. Ariaal will also eat cattle or camels which have died from predation or disease.

Although I did not measure actual consumption of food by individuals or households, I estimated average household and *per capita* consumption

Table 3.5 Contribution of Livestock Products to Ariaal Household Nutrition

	Camels	Cattle	Small Stock	Total	Total/Person
No. Owned/Household [a.]	16.5	22	80.5		
TLUs/household [b.]	20.6	22	7.3	49.9	8.2
Milk yields (l/day) [c.]	6.2	3.2	3.6	12.9	2.1
Milk calories (kcal/day)	4319	2268	2464	9051	1484
Milk protein (g/kg)	234.5	123.1	133.8	491.4	80.6
Meat yields (kg/day) [d.]	0.26	0.57	0.22	1.05	.17
Meat calories (kcal/day)	384.8	843.6	325.6	1554	254.8
Meat protein (g/kg/day)	57.2	125.4	48.4	231.0	37.9
Blood yields (l/day) [e.]	0.27	0.36	0.06	0.69	0.11
Blood calories (kcal/day)	89.1	118.8	19.8	227.7	37.3
Blood protein (g/kg/day)	21.6	28.8	4.8	55.2	9.04

Total livestock calories/person/day	1776 kcal
Total livestock protein/person/day	127.5 g
Additional calories/person/day : maize [f.]	250
Additional calories/person/day : sugar	227
Additional protein/person/day : maize	6.7
Total calories/per/day	2252 kcal
Total protein/per/day	134.2 g

a. 1 household = 6.1 persons

b. 1 TLU (total livestock unit) = 1 250 kg cow, 0.8 camel, or 11 small stock (Field and Simpkin 1985:170).

c. One liter of milk produces 700 kcal of energy and 38 grams protein. Milk yields are based on Dahl and Hjort's (1976:175,197,219) estimates:

camels - 34% total herd are fertile females, 50% of which are lactating, yielding an average of 2.2 liters milk daily for human consumption;

cattle - 29.5% herd fertile female, 50% lactating average 1.0 liter daily;

small stock - 35% flocks fertile females, 50% lactating average of 0.25 l daily.

d. Meat yields are based on UNESCO-IPAL estimates that Rendille consume 6% cattle herds, 3% camels, and 10% small stock annually. Dressed weight is 200 kg camels, 160 kg cattle, and 10 kg small stock, with 1 kg of meat equal to 1480 kcal and 220 g protein (Simpkin 1985:99).

e. Blood yields are based on estimates that 10% of each household herd is bled monthly, yielding 5 liters per large stock animal and 2 liters per small stock. Blood equivalences are 330 kcal/liter and 80 g protein/liter (Dahl and Hjort 1976:172-174).

f. Maize consumption is estimated at an average of 3.0 kg per household per week, and sugar at 2.5 kg/household/week, based on IPAL (1985:395) estimates that Rendille households consume of 4.5 kg of maize in dry season, 1.2 kg maize in the wet season, and 2.5 kg of sugar in both wet and dry seasons. Maize equivalences are 3560 Kcal/kg and 95 g/ kg; sugar is 3870 kcal/kg and 0 g protein/ kg (Field and Simpkin 1985:170).

of milk, meat, blood, and purchased foods based on herd size and productivity. Table 3.5 lists the estimated caloric and protein contribution of Ariaal herds to human nutrition.

From average household herd productivity, one estimates Ariaal to have access to 2252 Kcalories and 134 grams of protein per person per day from the milk, meat, and blood, and trade of their livestock. These figures are higher than reported for Turkana[16] and Rendille,[17] and closer to the WHO's Recommended Dietary Allowance (RDA) of 2800 kcal per adult male and

Figure 3.4. Milk and Maizemeal Consumption, Nomadic versus Mission Communities

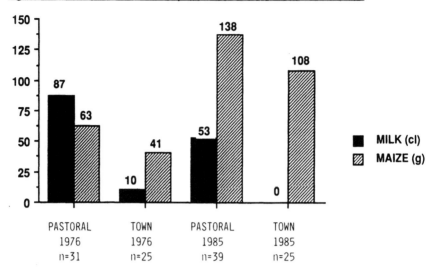

2000 kcal per adult female. The protein intake for Ariaal (and for other subsistence pastoralists) exceeds the WHO recommended protein allowances of 65g per adult male and 50g per adult women per day.[18]

Again, these figures estimate average and not actual differences in food consumption. Ariaal with adequate herds generate sufficient livestock products which offer a nutritional diet, providing adequate calories and more than adequate protein. While there are some mineral deficiencies, particularly iron, essential vitamins are obtained from the milk and blood. Despite seasonal shortages and differential consumption patterns, Ariaal livestock economy provides perhaps the optimum subsistence system available within this desert environment. Figure 3.4 shows milk and maizemeal consumption between pastoral (nomadic) and town (mission) Ariaal households for 1976 and 1985. While Ariaal had more milk in 1976 than the drought period of 1985, the pastoral communities had greater milk and maizemeal supplies in both periods compared to the poorer town residents who had few animals to trade for grains.

However, it is apparent that wealthier households with larger absolute numbers of livestock have better nutritional resources than poorer households. Rendille households need about 30 tropical livestock units to generate enough milk, meat, and trade for grains to satisfy minimum caloric intakes of 2300 kcal per person daily.[19] More than 35% of Ariaal households had this number of total livestock units, and it is these poorer households who have migrated to mission centers distributing famine foods.

While there is no direct evidence of protein-energy malnutrition (kwashiorkor or marasmus) among Ariaal, medical reports show that town dwellers may have lower nutritional status than the pastoral communities among Rendille.[20] In a recent study of settled Rendille living off famine-relief foods at Korr, Martha Nathan and I found lower hemoglobin levels in children under five years than among the pastoral communities.[21] It is unclear if the town-dwelling children suffered greater morbidity than the pastoralist children, although their mortality is lower due to their better access to medical care. Child mortality (0–5 years) among Kenyans in general is high (15/ 100) due mainly to infectious diseases such as malaria, measles, pneumonia, and to gasteroentiritis.

Summary

The relationship of pastoralists to their livestock herds is a complex one and determines much of the character of their society. The society organizes both household production and settlement organization around the needs of their livestock. The division of herds into domestic milk stock and surplus animals which can be grazed in distant camps demands a structured but flexible division of labor. Households share labor in the camps, but are independent in terms of herding and marketing decisions.

It is apparent from this description that Ariaal pastoral practices and strategies are the result of long-term adaptations to arid lands, and are not wasteful, ignorant, or short sighted. The various herds have their own grazing and water requirements, and each in turn provide calories, protein, and surplus for trade to their herders. The fates of human herders and their livestock populations are interlinked, and the herder is conscious of both short-term and long-term herding requirements for their animals.

Most importantly, the raising of domestic livestock for subsistence, particularly the raising of camels for milk and small stock and cattle for meat and exchange, is the most adaptive food production system in this arid environment. Agriculture, fishing, or hunting-gathering as food strategies cannot support as many people as livestock pastoralism in this region. It therefore appears ironic, if not sinister, that development agencies consciously have sought to alter this traditional subsistence system to suit the needs of the market.

Notes

1. IPAL 1984:34.
2. Descriptions of Marsabit vegetation resources are reported in IPAL 1984.
3. Carles 1980; Field 1985; Rutagwenda 1985; Schwartz 1979, 1980b.
4. McCabe 1987b.
5. Dahl and Hjort 1976.
6. Schmidt-Nielsen 1964:53–63.
7. IPAL researchers showed these camel milk yields could increase nearly 100% if adequate veterinary care was available, particularly that reducing internal worm loads. (Field and Simpkin 1985; Rutagwenda 1985, Schwartz 1980b; Wilson et al. 1979).
8. Field and Simpkin 1985:186.
9. IPAL 1984:268.
10. This practice in Turkana of using dogs to lick feces from infant children leads to a high incidence of hydatid disease, a nematode parasite in humans transmitted

from dogs (Rees et al. 1974). Rendille, Ariaal, and Samburu do not have this disease, because they keep their dogs away from humans.

11. Fratkin 1987b for division of labor in herding camps.

12. For description of this stratified time-allocation study see Fratkin 1987a, 1989a.

13. It is estimated that milk obtained from pastoral production provides 75% of daily calories to pastoral Rendille (Field and Simpkin 1985:171–72); 60% of daily calories to the Pastoral Maasai, (Grandin 1988:7), 60–70% of daily calories to the Boran (Cossins 1985:10), and 62% of daily calories (and 88% of daily protein) to the Turkana (Galvin 1985). In her study of nutrition among Ngisonyoka Turkana, Galvin (1985) found that livestock products provided 80% of dietary energy and 91% of daily protein, with milk consumption accounting for 62% and maize 24% of daily calories.

14. Rendille camel herds produce an average of 2.2 liters of milk per household for human consumption daily, ranging from 2.07–2.81 in the wet season and 0.92–1.52 liters in the dry season (Field and Simpkin 1985:181; O'Leary 1985:90). An average Ariaal household herd has 2.9 milk camels for 8 people, producing 0.8 liters of milk per person.

15. Schwartz 1979:161.

16. Turkana consumption: 1325 kcal/day/adult male (Galvin 1985).

17. Rendille consumption: 1875 kcal/day/adult male (Field and Simpkin 1985.)

18. WHO 1965.

19. Field and Simpkin (1985:171–72) estimate a Rendille household of 6.5 adults need 27–31 Total livestock units to provide enough calories and protein for its members.

20. Kadenyi 1983; Wiseman 1977.

21. Nathan and Fratkin 1990.

Household and Settlement: Inequality and Egalitarianism in Ariaal Life

4 There are several ways to enter a discussion of Ariaal social organization. If we are interested in formal structures organizing the society as a whole, then we need to focus our attention on descent organization, age set systems, and the political dominance of male elders over women and youth. If however we are concerned with daily economic life and social interaction, we must focus on households and the local group. Although lineage and clan affiliation in large part determine the composition of an Ariaal community, descent groups in themselves do not organize daily life. Being in the same lineage or clan does not guarantee cooperation or even interaction among its members—indeed some of the strongest conflicts in Ariaal arise between brothers. An Ariaal settlement is an autonomous cluster of individual households interacting on a regular basis. These local groups may or may not be permanent in composition and structure.

Local groups or settlements (the Samburu word *nkang*, meaning "ours," better connotes its sense of family and community) are composed of patrilineally related men and their families living in independent households but cooperating in larger processes of ritual, political, and economic life. An Ariaal household can be defined as the smallest domestic group with its own livestock and which makes decisions over allocation of labor and livestock capital.[1] Households are typically headed by a married male stockowner and include his wife or co-wives, children, and occasionally a dependent mother-in-law or married daughter who has not yet joined her husband's village. Each married woman is responsible for building and maintaining her own house; consequently an individual household may consist of three or four houses including two co-wives, a widowed mother, or a poor affine (in-law) and their children. A widow with unmarried children would constitute her own household as long as she held trust over her husband's herd; once her sons marry however they create their own households with the mother and remaining unmarried children dependent on the new household head.

Life in the settlements revolves around daily herding needs of the domestic livestock. Individual households cooperate extensively with each other in watering and grazing of their herds, both from the domestic settlements and in the distant livestock camps. Several households may combine their animals in common enclosures in the settlement (although each household maintains its own gateway), and different household labor forces may join together in mutual assistance. Sometimes one family may be poor in milk stock but have a sufficient labor force of adolescents, while other households may have small labor forces and too many animals to manage by themselves. In these cases, families hire poor relatives to herd their animals, paying one heifer cow or camel to boys working in the satellite camps for one year, or one small stock to younger boys or girls helping herd small stock near the domestic settlement.

Despite an appearance of homogeneity and conformity, Ariaal households display great variation in size and composition of their members and their wealth in numbers and types of livestock owned. Due to both changes in the developmental cycle of the domestic group and actual differences in inherited and acquired wealth, there exists a range of differences in wealth, where poor households may not have enough animals to feed their members, and wealthy households may lack adequate labor to manage all their animals.

Among pastoral Ariaal, kinship obligations provides a context for sharing, leading to a redistribution of milk animals with wealthy families loaning animals to poorer kin. Furthermore, households create cooperative herding arrangements to accommodate variations and shortages in livestock and/or labor, such that those families with too few children or laborers can foster or hire other children to herd their animals in exchange for livestock gifts.

Derek Stenning, who studied the pastoral Fulani of West Africa, defined "pastoral household viability" as an ideal ratio of household labor to pastoral herd size, "when the size and increase of the herd is adequate for the subsistence of the family and the size and composition of the family are suitable for the control and deployment of the herd."[2]

Gudrun Dahl, in her study of the Waso Boran of Kenya, defines the mechanisms with which the Boran households solve the problems of "non-viability": if a household has too few animals and too many people, it may (a) borrow milk stock from wealthier kin; (b) send excess labor away, either to herd for wealthier families, or to migrate to urban centers in search of wage labor; (c) merge one's herds with other families sharing the labor and food within the context of the livestock camps; or (d) a combination of any of these processes. Conversely, if the household size is too small to manage its animals, meaning in effect a wealthy but small family, it may, (a) merge its herds with another to share labor; (b) hire extra labor, usually from a large, poor, and related family within the settlement in exchange for payment in livestock; or (c) lend or place livestock elsewhere, usually with a relative in another settlement.[3]

These mechanisms are found among Ariaal. Households change in size and composition of their membership over time, reflecting the developmental cycle of the domestic group. A young newly wed couple will have few or no children, and must perform most of the herding, milking, and watering tasks. As the household matures, additional labor is generated by co-wives and adolescent children, offering the largest ratio of workers to the household. Finally as these children marry and begin their own households, the original couple (or surviving widow or less common widower) find declining labor again a problem, and will often become on their children's households.

It is common for a wealthy stockowner to hire a youth from poor but related households to herd his livestock in exchange for a female animal after a year's herding. Ariaal are not yet so integrated in the cash economy that wealthy stockowners end up living in town and paying wages for livestock herders as is now occurring among other groups such as the Waso Boran,[4] but there are nevertheless patron-client relations between wealthy and poor households in Ariaal. There is a tension within pastoral society that pits local solidarity and reciprocity (based on kinship ties of descent and marriage) against the competition and rivalry between individual households generating their own independent surplus of animals. It is, I believe, along these lines between wealthy and poor households that an incipient stratification develops within the society, and which can develop into class boundaries when wage and market relations are introduced.

Lewogoso Lukumai Settlement

Lewogoso Lukumai is typical of the large lowland Ariaal clan settlements. It is a large circle (or several circles depending on the year and season) of dome shaped houses surrounding livestock enclosures for camels, cattle, goats, sheep and donkeys. In 1974 Lewogoso members lived in one settlement of fifty houses with over 250 people, 600 camels, 800 cattle, and 2000 goats and sheep. The settlement was located at the eastern base of the Ndoto Mountains, about 15 km south of the Ngurunit wells and 12 km north of the Milgis River. When I returned in 1985, the people of Lewogoso were in the same area but had separated into three smaller circles located within 5 kilometers of each other, with those households with fewer loading camels living closer to the Ngurunit wells. Residents in all three communities expressed the desire to come together again when grazing conditions improved, but this had not occurred even by 1990.

In 1985, the resident population of Lewogoso was 269 in 58 houses. Demographically, the age-distribution of the settlement in 1985 was very similar to that in 1976, with a mean age of the settlement in 1985 of 25.6 years, compared to 1976 of 23.8 years. Figure 4.1 shows the population pyramids for Lewogoso in 1976 and 1985.

The average Lewogoso household has 1.6 houses, each occupied by a women (either the wife, the mother, or the mother-in-law of the household's male stockowner). The average number of residents per house in Lewogoso in 1985 was 4.3, which included children who were away in livestock camps, at school, at wage-jobs, or fostered to other families to help herd their

Figure 4.1. Population Pyramids of Lewogoso Lukumai Settlement, 1976 and 1985

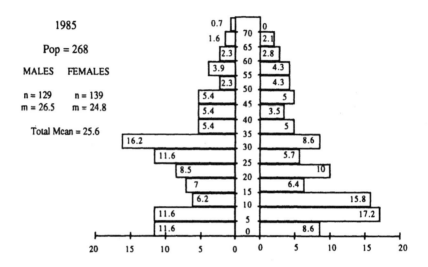

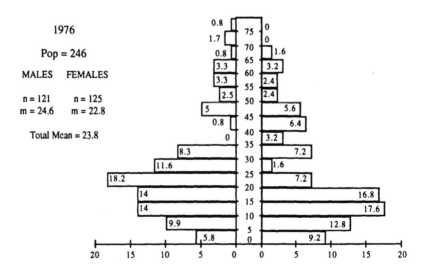

Table 4.1 Membership in Lewogoso Lukumai Settlement, 1976 and 1985

	1976	1985
Resident Stockowners	38	40
Close Agnates (same clan)	27 (71%)	30 (75%)
Distant Agnates	5 (13%)	3 (7.5%)
Affinal Kinsmen	3 (8%)	5 (12.5%)
Friends	3 (8%)	2 (5%)

livestock. It did not include daughters who have married out to other settlements. Actual residents per house, excluding those children at school, employed wage labor, or loaned to other families, was 4.0 of whom 2.4 were children under eighteen years of age.

Ariaal households are small, with only 13.9% having 5 children or more, 17.2% with 3 to 4 children, and fully 56.2% having fewer than 3 children each resident at home.

Settlement Recruitment

Ariaal settlements such as Lewogoso are ideally composed of members of one patrilineal descent group, that is, male members and their families belonging to Lewogoso clan of Lukumai section of Ariaal. Wives, although married into the settlement, do not belong the clan, but retain their descent affiliation with their father's clan located elsewhere, providing an important link to non-descent group kin. All children are members of their father's descent group.

In addition to descent-based stockowners, Ariaal settlements will also have stockowners related more distantly, including Rendille from agnatically related clans such as Tubsha for Lewogoso, or by affinal ties created through marriage. Some residents may not be related by any kin ties, but may be there by virtue of friendship with particular male stockowners. Ariaal in fact have a history of absorbing immigrants from many quarters, and different families attribute origins to a variety of cultures including Rendille, Samburu, Boran, Turkana, Dasenech (called Reshiat in Ariaal), Elmolo, Meru, and Maasai (particularly the Laikipiak). An Ariaal settlement may typically contain 20–25 percent non-clansmen as resident stockowners, as shown below in Table 4.1.

A small but significant number of the settlement's population are those related by marriage ties, that is, sons-in-law and brothers-in-law residing with their wives' patrilineal family. Occasionally these living situations are temporary, such as when a newly-married husband from another clan lives in the settlement for six-months or so, contributing labor to his father-in-law until his wife has recovered from the circumcision operation performed at her wedding. More often these non-lineal men are Rendille who move into an Ariaal settlement to seek better opportunities in raising livestock than those offered in their own settlements. Rendille acquire livestock principally through primogeniture inheritance, with younger sons receiving no livestock save a few cattle or small stock given as gifts, the bulk of the camel herds going to the oldest brother. These Rendille may then join Ariaal in the hopes of building up their small stock and trading for cattle.

In one case, an eldest son among a Rendille family joined his widowed sister in Lewogoso Lukumai, bringing along his young wife and widowed mother. This Rendille elder had a cattle herd of forty head in addition to a sizable camel herd, but with no children to herd the animals. Although the cattle (gained from raids against the Turkana) had been in his family for three generations, they had previously been managed by Ariaal affines on Marsabit Mountain. He chose permanent residence among Ariaal to utilize his widowed sister's children as labor, and to provide better pasture for his cattle. Joining Ariaal was a move by this elder to increase his cattle herd directly by his own management, without forsaking his camels herds.

An individual may join Ariaal even if he has no previous relationship with the settlement based on descent, marriage, or age-set ties. Such was the case of Arge, a Rendille of the junior elder age-set, the *Kishili*. Having developed a positive relationship with a Lewogoso elder based on joint wage work in Marsabit, Arge moved into Lewogoso in 1976 with his wife and mother in order to build up his cattle herds. By 1985, he had increased his herds from 24 cattle to over 100, had gained a second wife, and enlarged his family from 1 to 8 children. Although still friendly with Lewogoso, he had moved out of the settlement and into Ngurunit town, where he worked for UNESCO-IPAL herding livestock, while independently engaging in his own livestock transactions in the cash market. By 1990, Arge's family had grown to three wives and twelve children. In addition to livestock transactions, he conducted camel-back tours for tourists and was in the process of opening a shop. Arge stands at one end of the Ariaal scale, a self-made man who was able to build up his own herds and family. At the other end of the scale lie those Ariaal with no or few animals, many of whom also end up in Ngurunit town searching for the few wage jobs or even becoming *Dorrobo*, poor people who hunt and collect honey in the mountains. Despite is appearance of homogeneity, Ariaal is a varied and heterogeneous society in terms of wealth measured by livestock holdings.

Cooperative Herding Groups

Within the pastoral settlements, households join together to form cooperative units which share mutual production tasks. Cooperation among households may be organized by direct kinship ties, or by individual choice independent of kinship relations and based on compatibility and mutual need. Whereas descent and marriage ties are permanent, cooperative herding groups, whether based on kinship or not, tend to be less permanent and fluctuate according to the particular needs of households for labor or access to milk stock.

Figure 4.2. Lewogoso Lukumai Settlement and Internal Herding Groups, 1976

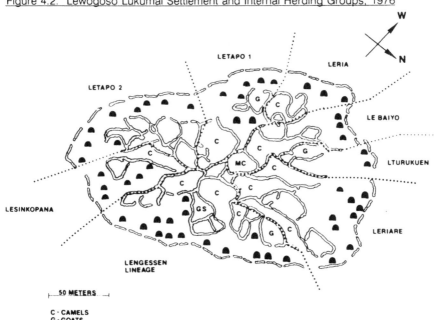

C - CAMELS
G - GOATS
GS-GOATS SLEEP
MC-MEN'S CTR.

Often lineage groups form the basis of co-residence, when members build their houses side by side, and herd their animals together. Members of a lineage trace descent to a common ancestor and share common family names. Often members of the same lineage build their houses together and share herding labor, but this is not always the case, particularly if full or half brothers do not get along with each other. Lewogoso settlement is organized predominately by lineage groupings, as show in Figure 4.2. The major lineage groupings in Lewogoso are Lengesen, Leriare, Letapo, Lenkiribe, Lenampere, Lebaiyo, Lesinkopana, and Leboinyo.

The membership of cooperative herding groups changes over time, as conditions of household and settlement change. In 1976, for example, three married brothers of the Lengesen lineage herded their livestock together, sharing their young labor force. In addition to the three brothers, an unrelated friend, the *loiboni* Leaduma, shared his few livestock in the same enclosures. Next to this enclosure was that of co-lineage agnates, the Lenampere family which consisted of a four households of nine houses including a married son-in-law, Lepasile, and a brother-in-law, Legombe. By 1985, these households had separated into seven different herding groups, living in four different locations. The kinship diagram of this lineage in 1976 appears in Figure 4.3.

Lineage affiliation is no guarantee that members will form cooperative herding groups, or even get along with each other. Sometimes close lineage

Figure 4.3 Lengesen Lineage and Household grouping   1976

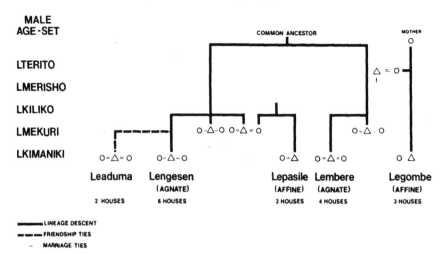

LINEAGE DESCENT
FRIENDSHIP TIES
MARRIAGE TIES

ties result in rivalry and competition, with brothers separating from each other and even moving to separate settlements. This happened in a situation in which two brothers, both in the Mekuri elder age-set, had a continuous rivalry based ultimately on the younger brother's success in stock management, which made him the wealthier of the two. Furthermore, the younger brother had two wives, while the older had only one. In one particular incident that led to their separation, the older brother ordered his brother's younger wife to run errands for him at Ngurunit, a distance of 15 kilometers. When the younger brother returned home to discover his wife gone, he shouted at his older brother not to interfere with him or his household. In response, the older brother beat the younger one with a stick, causing bloodshed. Overt violence between kinsmen is frowned upon in Ariaal, and the elders disapproved of what the older brother did. But they publicly upheld seniority and fined the younger man for shouting at his brother. Privately, however, the settlement elders agreed with the younger brother's actions, and the older brother, disgraced, moved away and joined another clan settlement.

Variation in Household Wealth

Cooperative herding groups are formed when a household has either insufficient stock to feed its members, in which case it merges with or donates its labor to a wealthier house; or when a household has insufficient labor to manage its livestock. These arrangements reveal a situation not generally discussed in studies of traditional pastoral economies, that of wide differences in wealth and property among pastoralist households.

Dahl's ethnography of the Waso Borana,[5] neighbors of Ariaal to the south, is one of the first to discuss wealth differences among East African

Figure 4.4 Total Livestock Units per Household, Lewogoso Lukumai 1976-1985

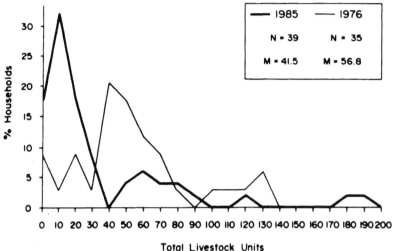

pastoralists, noting that the ethos of egalitarianism masks the real wealth differences within the society. The same holds for Ariaal. Sixty six percent of Lewogoso households have fewer than 30 total livestock units (TLU's), while 4.0% have more than 80 TLU's. (A tropical or total livestock unit" is defined as one 250 kg cow, 0.8 camel, or stock.)[6] I conducted livestock counts in Ariaal mainly during rituals of *soriu* and *almhado*, when most of their animals were returned from the livestock camps for blessings. These counts unfortunately do not distinguish between those animals owned and those borrowed from other families.

Figure 4.4 shows wealth differences in Lewogoso of total livestock units per households, comparing the rates of 1985 to 1976. As can be seen, there was a decline of total stock for the entire settlement, with a mean ownership of 56.8 units per household in 1976, and 36.1 units per household in 1985. This reflects the large scale of loss of livestock, particularly cattle and small stock, during the drought of 1982–1984. The figure also shows that while more households had larger herds in 1976, the number of households with more than 80 livestock units increased by 1985. This implies an increased polarization of wealth following the drought, a development which is discussed further in Chapter 6.

When we distinguish different categories of livestock, as in Figures 4.5, 4.6, and 4.7, it is clear that cattle losses were greatest during the drought, small stock showed heavy losses but recovered quickly, and camel ownership remained fairly stable. This is due fundamentally to the camel being a drought-adapted animal, while cattle are extremely dependent on stable water and grazing resources. Significantly, small stock flocks recovered quickly (owing to high reproductive rates) and represent an important form of insurance against drought or other large-scale losses.

Figure 4.5 Cattle Ownership in Lewogoso Lukumai, 1976-1985

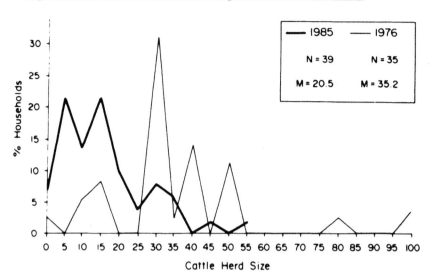

Figure 4.6 Camel Ownership in Lewogoso Lukumai, 1976-1985

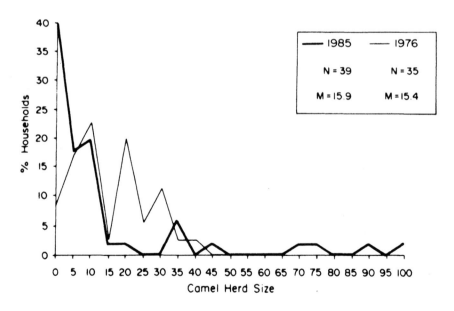

As shown, Ariaal households vary in wealth, measured in types and quantity of livestock owned. Households can be categorized as rich, middle, or poor, based on both how Ariaal rank each other, and objective ranking based on *per capita* herd size. I ranked wealthy households as those with more than 7 TLUs, middle as greater than 7 but less than 4, and poor

Figure 4.7 Small Stock Ownership in Lewogoso Lukumai, 1976-1985

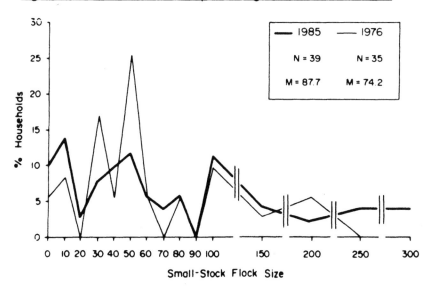

households as those with fewer than 4 TLUs per person. Four and one half TLUs is considered the minimum required to produce approximately one liter of milk per day per person, which as described in the last chapter, is a minimal daily nutritional requirement.[7]

Based on this criterion of Lewogoso wealth, 32 percent of Lewogoso's forty eight households in 1985 were considered rich, 23.5% were middle, and 44.5% were poor. When drought occurred in 1982–1984 it was the poor who were driven into destitution and sought famine relief in the missions, for a man with 50 cattle can lose 75% of his stock but recover; a man with 10 cattle may never recover from such a loss. Ariaal stockowners constantly reminded me that a rich man can survive livestock losses to drought, disease, or theft much better than a poor man, and wealth in livestock is seen as the main strategy with which to survive catastrophic losses.

Household variation in wealth, size, and the type of livestock raised affect the amount of labor each household member must perform. In 1985 I conducted time-allocation surveys consisting of spot checks unannounced to different households. I and my assistants noted the task activity, gender and age of every person we witnessed. After several weeks and 4000 observations, we came to the several conclusions. Members from poor households concentrating on small stock work more intensely than wealthy households concentrating on large stock. Furthermore in all households rich and poor alike, married women worked harder than married men and had one third less time for rest and leisure than married men. The following Figures 4.8 and 4.9 compare time allocations by men and women stratified

Figure 4.8 Task Performances of Ariaal Men, Stratified for Wealth, Dependency Ratio, and Livestock Specialization

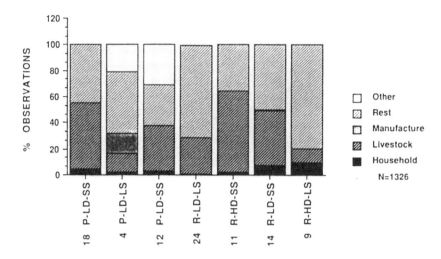

Figure 4.9 Task Performances of Ariaal Women, Stratified for Wealth, Dependency Ratio, and Livestock Specialization

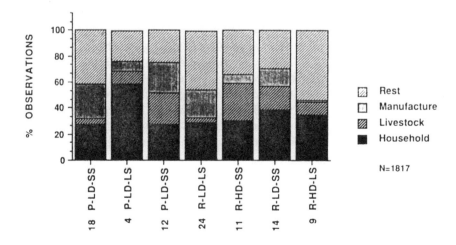

for wealth (Poor or Rich), household dependency ratio (High or Low), and whether they specialize in Large stock or Small stock.[8]

There has been considerable debate among anthropologists over the question of inequality in subsistence economies and whether exploitation exists in kinship-based, non-class societies. In particular, this debate has focused on the oppression of women.

The Status of Women

Ariaal women play a considerable role in Ariaal economic production. Not only are women responsible for all domestic tasks of child-care, house maintenance, and cooking, they also carry out many livestock-associated tasks including herding as well as caring for pregnant cows and calves. Yet Ariaal women (like Maasai, Samburu, and Rendille) cannot own livestock. Although women receive a herd of milk stock from their husbands at marriage to feed the household, they cannot sell or give away these animals, nor can they build up herds of their own. The house and household equipment are the only assets that a woman owns (in the sense that she can produce and distribute these goods), but access to milk and other food products are ultimately controlled by men. While a widow can exercise some control over her deceased husband's herd, particularly when her children are small, this is only in trust until her male children are old enough to marry.

Ariaal women are essentially powerless in the society, as they own no independent property. Dependent on their fathers when children, and on their husbands as adults, women enter old age (and typically widowhood) dependent on sons to feed and care for them. Men, by virtue of their control of livestock capital, insure that the public and jural spheres are their exclusive domains as well. Male dominance over women is compounded by the large age difference between spouses at marriage. In 1985 the mean age of married men was 47 years, while the mean age of married women was 38.8 years. This nine year difference is due to the late marriage age of men who do not marry until the release from warriorhood in their mid-thirties. Women marry in their late teens to men at least fifteen years older than themselves. In polygynous unions, a young girl may marry a man in his sixties. Furthermore widows do not remarry in Ariaal, but become attached to the households of their sons or their husband's brothers. Due to the payment of bridewealth (usually eight cattle) to a woman's father, widows are not permitted to remarry or return to their natal home. Divorce is also discouraged by a woman's family, who are reluctant to return the bridewealth.

A widowed woman consequently continues to reside in the clan settlement of her husband. The institution of levirate fatherhood (where men father children from their brother's widow) insures continued male control of not only a woman's productive labor but reproductive power as well. Reproductive labor includes both the social reproduction of the household through nurturing and child care as well as the actual biological reproduction of potential heirs and household labor. Women's ability to produce children and thus expand the household labor force strikes me as a leading reason to uphold polygyny as an ideal for married men. Although polygyny may not affect the fertility rate (some studies suggest polygyny may actually decrease reproductive rate), male elders can obtain more labor—both from women and their future children—through multiple marriages. The polygyny rate in Lewogoso in 1985 was 1.39, that is 100 married men have 139 wives between them, where almost one half of the married men have more than one wife. A few wealthier men have three wives each.[9]

Polygyny is valued by both men and women in Ariaal society for its contribution to the labor supply. Men state that polygyny means they can have more children to herd animals, and women prefer having a co-wife with whom to share household tasks. However, it is also apparent that polygyny and Ariaal marriage customs are a source of women's oppression, where a woman trades the authority of her father for that of her husband.

A woman seldom chooses her husband and is not party to the marriage negotiations. Her prospective spouse (whom she may or may not know) declares his marriage intentions to the girl's father and his patrilineal kin, using an intermediary (a brother or close friend) to make the initial approach. If the girl's family agrees to the union, negotiations over bridewealth are made. Ideally this should include eight cattle, one of which is killed and eaten during the wedding ceremony, but most marriage payments are a combination of small stock (goats and sheep), large stock, and occasionally cash, paid out over a long period and even into the next generation.

On the wedding day the groom and his best man present the wedding ox to the bride's father, having carefully guarded the ox on the previous night to prevent elopement (if a suitor kills the wedding ox before the groom does, he may "take" the bride as his own). While the groom and his people ritually kill the ox (by puncturing the base of the skull with a knife), the girl is undergoing female "circumcision"—an operation in which the local midwife cuts and removes the clitoris (clitoridectomy) and often the labia majora. Showing extraordinary fortitude, the bride will come out of the house in a few hours to greet the guests at the wedding who have been feasting on the wedding ox.

Ariaal women showed surprise and disdain when I told them we do not circumcise women in my country. The wife of one elder told me in consciously contradictory terms,

> "It is bad that you don't circumcise women in your country. That child which is born to such a woman, is it human? We think it is bad to bear a child if the woman is not circumcised. But you know, the men like to see us circumcised. They think we won't see other men if we are circumcised. But they are wrong," she laughed.

Ariaal women endure male domination in both ideology and control of economic resources. There was an exceptional case in Lewogoso of powerful and independent woman, however. A wealthy widow whose husband died when she was young managed her household herds until her children had grown. Although she did not own these animals in a strict sense, she engaged in most husbandry decisions (deciding which animals to breed) as well as managed the sales of her livestock. Maintaining a reputation as a shrewd and responsible stock keeper, this woman often participated in discussions with Lewogoso elders over grazing decisions, where and when to move the settlement, and political questions relating to the larger government. This was done privately however, and not in the usual context of men's discussions in their shade area or in the men's ritual center, the *na'apu*.

Control of Youth by the Elders

French anthropologist Pierre-Phillipe Rey[10] argues that there exists exploitation of juniors by male elders in kinship societies, particularly as the elders exercise jural and political control by restricting access of young men to marriageable women. Paul Spencer argues from a different perspective that Samburu elders maintain their age-set system and its institutionalization of warriorhood in order to remove the warriors from the marriage pool for a fourteen year period, permitting the elders to practice polygyny on a wide scale.[11]

Certainly among Ariaal it is clear that members of the warrior age-set as well as adolescents in general work long and hard hours in livestock production, while their fathers work considerably less in these arduous activities, but I am not convinced that this involves appropriation of the juniors' labor power as Rey argues. Youth are not irreversibly exploited by the elders; rather the livestock produced by the youth's labor, is ultimately returned to them through the redistributive processes of Ariaal economy, particularly by inheritance. Although most of the inheritance of livestock passes to the eldest son, this is never exclusively so, as a male stockowner seeks to disperse his livestock holdings over a larger geographic and social area, often giving gifts of livestock to different sons over the course of their lives.

One could argue that it is the older brother who appropriates the labor of his younger brothers, as in the case of a young elder using his warrior brothers to herd his livestock. But male herders do receive returns, immediate or delayed, for their labor in the form of gifts, direct payments, and inheritance.

This is qualitatively different from the situation of women, who receive no livestock or other products in exchange for their labor. Furthermore, the product women help produce—livestock—have exchange-values as well as use-values. Livestock are not only "used" to feed the domestic group, they are also exchanged on the cash market for other livestock, or through the traditional sphere as bridewealth for other wives. While it can be argued that foods bought with livestock sales are a form of "use-values" returned to women, the exchange values—and the fact that men can buy more livestock and labor for their own exclusive use, implies appropriation of the woman's labor for men.

Ariaal is not a class-based society, at least not in its internal relationships. Elders no more constitute a fixed "nonproducing" class than youth and warriors form an impoverished "producing" class. Nevertheless, elders do hold a privileged position in the society—they work less and own more than any other group. Furthermore, it can be argued that they do appropriate at least some of the product of their dependent juniors and women. An

Ariaal elder of Merisho age-set, 1975

essential feature of warriorhood, in addition to permitting polygyny by the elders as noted by Spencer, is the fact that the elders can expand and prolong their household labor by delaying the marriage of their warrior sons until their mid-thirties. In this way, Ariaal elders extend and maximize their domestic labor force, and ultimately satisfy their labor needs. However, where warriors become elders, women never do.

Patron-Client Relationships

Incipient stratification in the form of patron-client relationships has been noted in pastoralist societies, particularly in the Mideast and southwest Asia.[12] In these societies, mutually beneficial relationships are established between members of poor households and those of wealthier households, often in the context of ritual and kinship ties. Ultimately these relationships may translate into exploitative ones, if the wealthier households utilize the labor power of poorer households without returning an equivalent share of the product, or else acquire the land or property of poorer households through debt transactions.

Dahl[13] and Hjort[14] note a similar trend of class formation emerging among the Boran and Somali of Isiolo District in Kenya. Despite what Dahl refers to as an "ethos of egalitarianism", the Boran, like Ariaal, are a varied society with a great range in household wealth. Effected by drought, development, and the political turmoil of *shifta*, during which time the government confiscated much of their livestock, many Boran migrated to towns, seeking wage labor if poor, or entering the livestock market as entrepreneurs if wealthy or educated. In this situation, wealthy Boran stockowners could live permanently in town, hiring or otherwise utilizing poorer kin relations to herd their livestock. Ultimately, a new class of educated and more privileged entrepreneurs developed, with rural and poorer kin becoming proletarianized as wage-laborers.

The phenomenon of patron-client relations in Ariaal has not developed to the same degree as in Boran, yet they face the possiblity of a similar class formation. There are already relations of dependency between Ariaal households, where poorer relatives perform various tasks for wealthier stockowners in exchange for livestock. Although this appears to be a reciprocal relation, where the wealthier Ariaal offers payment in livestock or use of milk animals, it is not truly equal because the laborer seldom has a chance to build up large herds for himself. The situation is a bit different when Ariaal find wage work and rebuild their herds through the market; this situation is discussed in more detail in Chapter 6.

Wage-relations do not dominate Ariaal economy at this time, but the market economy is expanding into Ariaal, accelerated by the process of drought and national development plans. Ariaal society, traditionally divided into wealthier and poorer households, is experiencing a large fission between those who can remain in the livestock economy and those who cannot. Not all town dwellers are poor, however, as there is emerging a new elite of livestock traders, store owners, and a "salariat" of government-employed administrators drawn from the pastoralist community in both Ariaal and Rendille. As sedentarization and modern education proceed in northern Kenya, it appears that stratification within the formerly egalitarian Ariaal may well emerge as it has among other pastoralists engaged in the market economy.[15]

Notes

1. This definition of household follows Dahl 1979b:70.
2. Stenning 1959:100.
3. Dahl 1979b:81-85.
4. Dahl 1979a; Hjort 1981.
5. Dahl 1979b.
6. Field and Simpkin 1985:70.

7. Pratt and Gwynne (1977) used the formulation that 4.5 TLUs was minimum livestock necessary to sustain one person. We used this figure in our analysis of survivorship through drought of Ariaal Households. (Fratkin and Roth [In Press]).

8. Fratkin 1989b.

9. As discussed in Chapter 2, Ariaal and Samburu have higher polygyny rates than Rendille, who have a rate of less than 1.1, due to their use of cattle for bridewealth payments rather than camels. Camels have a lower reproductive rate than cattle, and formerly it was almost impossible for a Rendille stockowner to have more than one wife. However, an increase in cattle ownership among the Rendille is leading to a growing polygyny rate among Rendille men as well as Ariaal (Fratkin in press).

10. Rey 1979.

11. Spencer 1965.

12. Bradburd 1980:603; Salzman 1979:421.

13. Dahl 1979a:219.

14. Hjort 1979:90–98.

15. Bourgeot 1981.

The Impact of
the Christian Missions

5 After years of neglect by the colonial government, independent Kenya opened the northern districts to international agencies and private voluntary organizations to help with the country's development. Christian missionaries, particularly Catholic orders and the Protestant evangelical Africa Inland Church (AIC), wasted little time establishing missions in Samburu, Marsabit, and Turkana Districts.

At independence in 1963, Marsabit District's 80,000 people had only three primary schools educating one hundred students, no secondary schools, and only one government hospital. The Kenya government under Jomo Kenyatta, however, did not invest heavily in the north, allocating the lion's share of western aid to the populated regions of the central highlands and the coast. Much of the development of Marsabit District's schools, medical dispensaries, and water resources were undertaken by international donors, principally by the Christian missions. The government did, however, build and maintain the hospitals and secondary schools at Marsabit and Moyale.

After years of sitting on the sidelines of missionary activity in Kenya, the Catholic Church and AIC flourished in the north after independence. Catholic missionaries from Italy, Holland, and Ireland as well as Protestant fundamentalists from the United States and Canada had been active in Kenya since the First World War, but they had been marginalized from the heavily populated areas, which were dominated by mainstream British missions, particularly the (Anglican) Church Mission Society and the (Presbyterian) Church of Scotland. Following independence and the decline of British influence, the Catholics and AIC developed missionary work throughout Kenya as a whole.[1]

Between 1954 and 1978 the Catholic Church established twelve missions (with churches, primary schools and dispensaries) in Marsabit and Samburu District.[2] After Kenyatta's death in 1978, President Daniel arap Moi (himself a product of AIC schools), allocated more resources to the pastoralist regions, and by 1980 the government was administering all primary schools and supervising the clinics, which were still run largely by the missions. By 1984 Marsabit District had three secondary schools, three hospitals, and over thirty primary schools.[3]

Missionary activity among Rendille and Ariaal of Marsabit District took off in a period of social and environmental disruption. The *shifta* war of the 1960s disrupted education, health care, and road building, and the droughts of the 1970s and 1980s produced a large number of destitute pastoralists seeking famine relief. Previous to the 1960's, pastoralists survived drought by traditional means such as moving to better pastures, but the presence of traditional enemies now armed with rifles forced groups like Rendille to confine their herding to narrow areas around fixed water points. The missions, established at these points, began engaging in large scale famine-relief after 1973.

Despite wide differences in ideology and organization, the Catholic Church and the AIC share a commitment (with the Kenyan government) to settling the pastoralists around the growing towns. Many missionaries share the view that pastoralism is primitive and irrational, and they hold paternalistic attitudes towards the pastoralists. A Catholic priest at the Korr Mission said,

"These Rendille are really children, here today, gone tomorrow. They have no roots, no home to call their own. Here (at Korr), they have for the first time a regular water supply, sanitary latrines, shops, schools, a dispensary. But they have a long way to go before they can be truly independent."

While they may have latrines at Korr, they do not have their animals. Before 1975, Korr was a seasonal water hole in the middle of the rocky and windblown Kaisut Desert, about sixty kilometers west of Marsabit town. Since the establishment of the Catholic Missions at Korr, Kargi and Laisamis, over 50% of the Rendille population have permanently settled without having daily access to their livestock. Many now look for scarce wage work or continue to receive assistance from the missions.

The Catholic Church

In sheer size, funding, and political clout the Catholic Church dwarfs other religious missions in Marsabit and Samburu Districts. The church has one dozen large missions in the region (each with a church, primary school, and dispensary), compared to four small AIC missions, and has funding sources vastly superior to the Protestant groups. Furthermore, the Catholic Diocese of Marsabit is a major participant in governmental discussions concerning development, education, and social services in the region.

Rendille have been affected by the Catholic missions to a much greater degree than Ariaal, in part because the Catholics established massive famine-relief efforts among Rendille in the 1970's some distance from the Ariaal. Ariaal have been more directly affected by the AIC mission than by the Catholic Church. Whether by chance or choice, the AIC have kept their distance from the Catholics. There has been a separation of "domain" between the Protestants among the Ariaal (at Ngurunit, Logologo, and Karare) and the Catholics among Rendille (at Korr, Kargi, and Laisamis), but owing to the growth in these towns the Catholics have built a primary school at Ngurunit and AIC have affiliated projects at Korr.

Rendille children and teachers at Korr Primary School, Korr Catholic Mission, 1990

The Catholic missionaries in Marsabit District come largely from Italy. In 1953 the Consolata Order built a church, dispensary and primary school in Marsabit town, and within fifteen years had built missions among Rendille and Ariaal at Laisamis and Archer's Post; among the Samburu at Baragoi, South Horr, and Maralel; among the Gabra at North Horr and Maikona; and Elmolo on Lake Turkana at Loiyengalani. More recently, Indian missionaries from Don Bosco Mission have joined the Korr Mission.

The philosophy and behavior of the Italian missionaries are remarkably similar to the "White Fathers" who missionized the Belgian Congo (Zaire) and East Africa at the end of the 19th century. Like their predecessors, the Consolata missionaries initially focused on developing closed environments ("ferme chapelle") consisting of bounded missions with boarding schools that would remove African youths from their traditional social environments, "incubating" them with the structure and customs of the church.[4]

The Catholic missions of northern Kenya invariably resemble each other, consisting of a large church with domestic quarters for priests, surrounded by separate staff housing for nuns and the African staff. The buildings are made of cinder block plastered white, with metal windows and corrugated steel roofs, and their architecture and even the gardens reflect the European origin of the missionaries. The missions are often walled or fenced in, with the school house, dispensary, or famine-relief distribution located outside the church compound. The missions are imposing and foreign structures to local populations such as Ariaal, and interaction between the missionaries and Africans is confined to Sunday mass in the cathedral and the distribution of services (education, health care, food-aid) at locations some distance from the church.

Mission centers have developed into rural towns with resident populations that include former pastoralists, shopkeepers, and government personnel such as police and district administrators. Pastoralists are attracted to the mission centers for many reasons. Most of the social services are provided by the missions, particularly health care, and there are shops in which to sell livestock and buy needed goods and food. Furthermore, the missions are invariably built at the permanent water sources, now mechanized by hand pumps or diesel engines.

The number of sedentarized pastoralists around mission centers grew enormously following the drought of 1968–1973, as the Catholic church in particular assumed responsibility for distributing relief grains of corn, rice, and soybean flour. Although these supplies were made available to the Kenyan Government by international relief agencies including USAID, UNICEF, and CARE, the Kenyan government often distributed these supplies through the missions who provided the vehicles and petrol.

As the 1970 drought intensified and famine conditions set in, the Catholic Church at Laisamis began mobile visits to water points distant from the Marsabit road, distributing famine foods to pastoral Rendille at the wet season watering holes of Korr and Kargi in the Kaisut Desert. By 1973, permanent missions were established at Kargi and Korr, which soon attracted an estimated 6000 Rendille, primarily women and children too small to herd livestock in distant camps. Catholic missions concentrated on welfare activities such as education and curative health services. While they did (and do), provide childhood vaccinations against measles, tetanus, and diphtheria to mothers and children who visited their clinics, they did not engage to any great degree in mobile health clinics to the more isolated areas, nor did they provide education or delivery of veterinary services for pastoral livestock. The main concern of the Catholic missions appeared to be establishment of large churches and encouragement of settled and dependent populations around the missions.

The Korr Catholic Mission

The largest settled Rendille population is at the Korr Catholic Mission, which in 1990 had a resident population of about 2500 people. Ironically Korr began as one of the most innovative and democratically run famine-relief projects of the Marsabit Diocese. Korr is a windblown and rocky area devoid of trees, but has permanent water found in subterranean wells along dry river beds. Prior to 1973, Korr was a seasonal Rendille watering hole where camels and small stock could water and graze on the temporary grasses of the Kaisut Desert before the dry season set in.

In the late 1960's, priests from the Catholic Church at Laisamis began regular trips to Korr to distribute famine grains as the drought crisis heightened. In 1971, a young Italian priest, Father Redento, began a permanent mission at Korr. At first Redento lived quietly among Rendille, visiting their camel camps and settlements and learning to speak their language. Within eight months, however, Redento had raised funds in Italy and mechanized the local boreholes, building a 1000 gallon storage tank which was pumped by a new windmill.[5] The creation of an accessible year-round water supply, as well as the regular distribution of famine-foods, attracted 400 Rendille families to this desert location, mostly married men, women, and small children, while adolescents and young adults herded the livestock in distant camps. The sparse resources of Korr however prevented residents from keeping milk animals in their settlements.

The Korr mission was a radical departure from more traditional Catholic missions at Laisamis and Marsabit. Redento's compound resembled a Rendille settlement, with staff and stores housed in Rendille-style domed houses built on wood frames covered by burlap bags; thorn bush enclosures surrounded vehicles rather than livestock. The church was a large oblong dome 20 meters long, constructed of burlap bags (from the famine relief foods) stretched over circular wooden frames. The floor and walls were covered in cowskins like a domestic Rendille house; at one end was a crude altar with a large crucifix, behind which were suspended twenty strands of ritual goatskin ropes normally worn by Rendille elders during the *soriu* and *almhado* rituals. Father Redento explained to me that the Rendille ritual paraphernalia were hung from the cross "to show Rendille that they no longer need to sacrifice goats for blessings, for God had sacrificed his only son for the salvation of all people."

Father Redento was very popular among Rendille at Korr; he was constantly on the move, greeting Rendille with warm handshakes as he scouted locations for wells, designed storehouses, or built roads. A large man with long hair and a beard, dressed in shorts, sandals and wearing Rendille beads, Redento was a far cry from the sedate priests in Marsabit. He was accessible to Rendille, and he could often be seen consulting with elders in Rendille language with which he had a reasonable fluency. Redento is still remembered fondly not only for his famine-relief efforts, but for incidents such as his challenging the strongest Rendille wrestler to a match, much to the delight of his Rendille hosts.

An elder who had lived in Korr since 1973 when Redento first arrived,

"The first time I came here, I was dying from hunger, I was so poor. I came to see Redento personally. I had no house even. I cut trees to make a shade. Redento gave me food, even if it was little, it was enough for me. Redento asked me what *almhado* was. I told him we take milk to the *na'apo* (ritual center) and bless all our people. Redento asked me where I would find milk without animals? I said we had no milk, so Redento said we can just use water. He mixed water with powdered milk and we were able to bless the village. Redento gave us a goat for *soriu*. When Redento left, we had very bad problems. Some people left and dispersed, but we remained like fish out

of water. Me, I 'prayed for daily bread' (i.e., I begged). . . . When Redento
was here, this place was beautiful."[6]

In 1974 Father Redento told me his story, in a practiced manner obviously
repeated to various journalists, as Redento had a keen eye for publicity and
fund-raising.

> "When I first came here three years ago, Rendille had hardly seen a white
> man. The first week I was here, I was put in with the camels to sleep. When
> I requested a hut, the elders discussed my case for four days. They finally
> agreed, telling me I am now one of them, but confessing at first that they
> were afraid of me, wondering 'where will he lead us?'" People would ask me
> what am I doing here, and I would respond 'what you see, that is what I am
> doing.' Soon they began calling me a 'man of God' and came to trust me.
>   "I didn't set up my church right away. In fact, for the first eight months, I
> lived as them, eating their food, joining in their rituals, learning the language.
> My first volunteer came just one year ago, when we're just two huts. I started
> introducing the mass, and even then we started slowly. Rendille have many
> stories out of the old testament: Adam and Eve, the woman coming from the
> man's right rib. Even now, a dead man is buried on his left side, to show
> that this where women came from. As we talked about these stories, I would
> tell them about Christ, that we don't have to sacrifice a goat, that God sacrificed
> himself. Initially we held a *soriu* ceremony every Sunday. We killed a goat
> every Sunday for a year until they asked me to stop killing the goat. They
> came to understand that Christ sacrificed his own self, and they didn't need
> to sacrifice a goat any more. That is why in the church now Christ hangs in
> front of the sacrifice stick, that He has replaced that stick."

Redento's mission attracted volunteers from Italy including health workers
and ecologists, journalists and artists. The mission had an atmosphere of
a utopian collective rather than a Catholic church. Redento was willing to
experiment and try any program he felt would aid his project. He opened
a community store to sell maizemeal, shoes, cloths, and beads at low cost
(transportation paid by the church); he developed a mobile dispensary to
make visits to distant settlements to bring sick Rendille to the Laisamis
hospital.
    Redento also established a "Korr Committee" consisting of a married
man and woman from each local Rendille settlement who met twice a
month to discuss mission projects including food distribution, water development, and interactions with the local Marsabit government. The committee radically departed from traditional "men only" discussions in Rendille,
but the men accepted this as a form particular to the mission, if not
necessarily one to repeat at home. Redento also trained 57 Rendille youth,
teens who had completed several years of school, and who were placed as
"catechists" in various Rendille settlements to preach the gospel and oversee
distribution of relief foods.
    Although Redento's methods were experimental and unorthodox compared
to the scrubbed order and disciplined hierarchy of other Catholic missions,

Redento's main business was nevertheless church business—the winning of converts to the Catholic faith. Redento baptized 250 Rendille, several of whom were selected to visit Pope Paul VI in Rome as part of a Kenyan delegation, creating an international press opportunity utilized by the Catholic Church and Redento himself.

Despite his good intentions and refreshing style of missionary work, Redento made little contribution to helping Rendille improve their livelihood or feed themselves. Although he installed an excellent network of catechists in the outlying settlements, Redento instituted no programs that would provide veterinary treatment of livestock, human vaccinations or other preventative medicines to children or pregnant mothers, or vocational education in livestock production to stock managers and owners. Despite the trucks owned and the roads constructed, there were no attempts to help Rendille market their livestock or form economic cooperatives, even though educated Rendille working in the mission stores urged the church to engage in this work.

Furthermore, despite his good intention, Redento had the same patronizing attitude towards Rendille that many other foreign missionaries held. Redento once told me,

"The Rendille are very primitive, they are really children. They look for today, for they have to eat. They are easy to 'get,' but they are easy to lose as well. The Boran are hard to get, but once you get them, they stick. They are much more individualistic than the Rendille."

Despite their easiness to "get," all was not smooth between Redento and the Rendille. In particular there were large struggles around Redento's control of the famine relief distribution. Many Rendille and Ariaal, particularly those from settlements not in Redento's orbit, accused Redento of hoarding famine-foods for his "own" Rendille. In fact, Redento had an ongoing arrangement with the overburdened Marsabit District relief personnel to use his truck and petrol to help distribute bags of maize, soy, and red beans stored in Marsabit town to Rendille at Korr.

When the drought intensified in 1975, elders from Lewogoso met with Redento after he delivered 720 kg of famine relief maizemeal to a neighboring settlement, but not Lewogoso, even though they were located four kilometers from each other. This food was provided by the government at Marsabit, and the elders wanted to know why none had been distributed to their village. Redento told them he could not distribute to them because they had no catechist and without one, Redento would not know who was poor and who was rich. An elder responded,

"How can an elder refuse his family (*nkang*, meaning all residents of the settlement) from eating?"

Redento defensively replied, "I'm sorry, but it is Marsabit and not me. We only have so much food for Korr and we can not give it out to anyone who asks for it, or we would have to feed all the Turkana and Boran. All we can do is to make sure the poor people, those in real need, will get some."

The elder responded, "This food is for all Rendille. I can tell you who is in need and who is not. But are you not saying that you will only give food to settlements who have catechists? Do you really wish to help those in need, or just those who follow the Catholics?"

Redento lost his temper and yelled, "All you want is free food! All you do is come here to beg from me, then behind my back you oppose me. Leave now, leave us to our work!"

The Lewogoso elders were shocked. Argument and debate are one thing, losing control and showing anger is another. They quietly discussed the matter among themselves, then approached Redento in a conciliatory manner, asking Redento to send Lewogoso a catechist "to make sure the poor people get food."

Redento softened and said, "We'll try a test case. If in two months the catechist tells us Lewogoso Lukumai is in need, we will send food then."

The elders left in disgust. After some more searching, they were able to bring back four bags of beans and corn maize on camel from the AIC mission at Ngurunit. The distribution procedure of the food at Lewogoso was public and highly egalitarian, with each married woman receiving the same two scoops (about two kg) of maize, enough to feed a household for about three days.

In the end it was not Redento's conflicts with Ariaal and Rendille that led to his downfall, but those with the Diocese in Marsabit. The Bishop of Marsabit opposed Redento's style and approach for some time, arguing that the mission was too chaotic, disorganized, and unstable. The Diocese was anxious to see construction of a permanent mission with a boarding school and a large church. Some critics suspected that the Bishop was concerned that Redento's radical policies would spread to other missions. In 1976 Redento was removed. He left Kenya and returned to Italy where he continued his social work in a rehabilitation program for drug addicts.

In 1980 Indian missionaries from the Don Bosco Mission (Silesian Order) took over Korr, and in time they built a permanent church, school, water tank, and dispensary. Famine food was distributed more selectively based on need (primarily to nursing mothers and destitute households), and a population of several thousand Rendille settled around the town center. Within a short time, Korr was transformed from Redento's temporary burlapped camp into a settled town with shops, permanent houses, and a local government.

The style of the Indian priests was quite different from that of Redento. Seldom leaving the mission compound, the priests focused on problems of institutionalizing the church, regularizing the mass, and constructing and running the primary school and dispensary. The character of the church changed as the character of the community had changed. Korr was no longer a community of impoverished Rendille waiting for food handouts but was now a permanent town with an established core of shops and

Korr Catholic Church after Sunday mass (from left to right: Annamarie Aliaro, Father George, Christina Mosodoge, Dr. Martha Nathan, and Sentarian Lekhoyan)

businesses. Church services were formal but nevertheless remained highly popular, with lively songs in Swahili and sermons in Rendille and Samburu. Korr had not taken on the seedy characteristics of Laisamis, whose church-built Sabamba village had become a home for beer-brewing and prostitution.

Despite its isolation and austere location, Korr is an energetic and future-oriented town. A number of primary and secondary school leavers are making their home there, hoping to engage in livestock marketing or to find jobs with government or development agencies. The Member of Parliament for Marsabit South is a young educated Rendille from Korr, and Korr residents have been active in local and county council elections. The church had ceased to be the center of the community, and Korr now has a life of its own.

The Africa Inland Church

The Africa Inland Church (AIC) is an evangelical Protestant organization made up of both African members and self-supporting missionaries from the United States, Canada, England, and elsewhere. Established in 1895 in Tanzania, the AIC spread to Uganda, Sudan, Zaire, and Kenya by 1924.[7] Today the AIC is mainly in Kenya with several dozen missions and a large headquarters, secondary school, and hospital at Kijabe outside Nairobi.

The AIC established missions in Marsabit District immediately after independence, largely through the efforts of the Anderson family. Missions were developed at Logologo below Marsabit town in 1963, at Gatab on Mt. Kulal in 1967, at Ngurunit along the Ndoto Mountains in 1971, with various projects in water development and agriculture at Songa, Nasikakwe, Illeret, Hurri Hills, Korr, and Marsabit town.

Ariaal and Rendille choir, AIC Mission at Ngurunit, 1985

Where the Catholic Church concentrated on creating large churches, primary schools, and distributing famine-relief, the AIC focused their efforts largely on water development. Many AIC missionaries are engineers and builders, directing much of their efforts at digging new wells, mechanizing water pumps, and building roads.

The development of water resources is an expensive endeavor, and it is understandable that the Kenyan government encouraged voluntary efforts such as the AIC for assistance. For example, in 1974 AIC missionaries from Logologo built the water pump at Gof Bongole in the Marsabit Reserve at a cost of $18,000, which went predominately to equipment (the pump, storage tank, trough, and tap), and transportation costs. While the funds are usually provided by the Kenyan government, the AIC have often provided technical assistance and transportation. Once built, the mechanized water pumps are maintained by the District Water Department, although AIC engineers are often called on to provide repairs and financial assistance.

The AIC's principal endeavor however is not water development, but religious evangelism. "The Africa Inland Church is first and foremost a religious group. Our main 'development' work is the development of local churches," wrote a local AIC missionary.[8] Invariably, the development of permanent water sources was accompanied by the construction of a church, primary school, dispensary, airstrip, and housing for the AIC missionaries.[9]

AIC missionaries are a hardworking, generous, and humble group of people, yet many remain ignorant of the local customs and practices of the people they endeavor to serve. While many missionaries form close working relationships with their African staff, few spend time in Ariaal settlements or attempt to understand Ariaal culture on its own terms. Their language study is mainly for bible translation (several missionaries are affiliated with the Summer Institute of Linguistics), although several AIC missionaries are learning Samburu and Rendille. Most are fluent in Swahili.

One AIC missionary spoke of how similar Rendille religion was to ancient Judaism:

> "The Rendille have a blood sacrifice in their *soriu* ritual which is really an atonement for sin, for breaking taboos. They mark their houses with the blood of the sacrificial lamb, just as the ancient Hebrews in Egypt did to protect against the angel of death; they also have an Exodus story and they believe in the return of the Messiah. The Rendille may be a degenerated form of the original Jewish tribe."

I asked this missionary if he ever witnessed a *soriu* ritual, because while it is true that blood is marked on living animals, it is milk that is poured on the house. I told him that I doubted that Rendille shared the Jewish belief in an angel of death, and I never hear of a belief in the messiah outside of converted Rendille. He replied that he had never actually witnessed a *soriu* ceremony, but believed the Rendille were related to ancient Hebrews. "Some things just change over time," he said.[10]

Like the Catholics, the AIC missionaries are a homogeneous and self-contained cultural group. Most missions are run by married couples who live with their children in contained mission compounds. Nearly all AIC missionaries are North American or English, and although many were born in Kenya or Tanzania, they maintain strong links to their own countries (each must spend a seventh year sabbatical raising funds). Furthermore the missions have a highly cohesive and internal network (missions communicate to each other daily by short-wave radio), and they maintain a unified culture with its own shared symbols, ideology, and even dialect. Weekly or monthly visits by airplane bring news and packages, and every mission home receives a turkey for Christmas. Their residences are microcosms of suburban America, with electric stoves, colonial furniture, and a myriad of mechanical or electric gadgets donated by congregations at home, powered by diesel generators and more recently, solar-powered batteries.

Married missionaries have a distinct division of labor; men engage in construction and operating machinery while women are responsible for nursing, teaching, and administrative tasks as well as for running the home and raising children. Men lead Sunday prayers, women run the Sunday schools.

The AIC has a large hospital near Nairobi where their local dispensaries can send seriously ill patients (often by airplane); (the Catholic Church in turn has a hospital at Laisamis and clinics at *their* local missions). The AIC clinics are fee-for-service. With classic display of the Protestant ethic, the AIC believe that paying for medicine, even if only a token shilling, leads Ariaal to an appreciation and willingness to work for goods and services, rather than "expect handouts". The AIC also maintain their own moral standards by charging considerably more for a penicillin shot used to treat gonorrhea than for a non-sexually transmitted infection.

The AIC's health care delivery is very good by rural Kenyan standards. They also engage in preventative medicine with mobile clinics visiting mothers and children in the Ariaal areas where AIC nurses administer measles, polio, and DPT vaccine (diptheria, pertussis, and tetanus).

The AIC is only marginally involved in famine-relief distribution. Although their missions occasionally distribute food aid donated by private groups such as World Vision, most famine relief in Marsabit is distributed through government offices or the Catholic Diocese. In part this is due to the sheer scale of the Catholic Diocese's organization compared to the AIC, but the differences in famine-relief policy also flow from ideological differences between the two missions.

Calvinist values of self-reliance, thrift, and saving inhibit the AIC from promoting food-aid dependency. "We want to make men of them, not babies," said an AIC missionary. Not surprisingly, the AIC have won few converts compared to the Catholic Diocese in Marsabit District, and they have not created large communities of dependent households. "We're not after numbers, its sincerity that counts."

A positive aspect of this outlook on self-reliance is the AIC's experimentation with programs in alternative food production including the introduction of irrigated maize agriculture at Songa on Marsabit Mountain and efforts to restock poor pastoralists with camels, goats and sheep. In the 1980s AIC missionaries at Korr and Ngurunit (as well as German Catholic missionaries among the Gabra at North Horr) initiated restocking programs and veterinary extension services funded by private religious groups and donations. More than any other service, it is these restocking efforts that Rendille see as the most direct benefit to their livelihoods. The Korr missionaries have provided animals to dozens of impoverished households, enabling people formerly driven out of the pastoral economy a chance to reenter it. A Rendille elder in his sixties, recounted his story in 1990:

"I've been at Korr eight years. I had a lot of problems on the lava (a herding area). Drought and disease finished my camels and I became very poor. I moved to Korr to find food and marry a second wife. I did not want to live in town, but my camels, cattle, goats, even the donkeys were finished. So I could not live outside town, I needed water, I needed help with food.

"Nick (Nick Swanepoel, a missionary affiliated with the Summer Institute of Linguistics and the AIC) came to our village, he went around from house to house to see how many animals we had. At first he gave us maizemeal, *kimbo* (cooking oil), powdered milk to every house, depending on the number of children. Nick fed people like this for two to three years.

"Nick was giving food to all of us at Korr. After some time, this stopped. Nick only visited these small villages around his place. He hired us for small jobs, particularly women to wash clothes, fetch water, plant trees. He paid them 300 shillings a month.

"Then Nick stopped these small jobs. He said 'We want to help you help your children so I will give you animals.' He wrote the name of every person and said, "I'll give you each a *panga* (machete), a cloth, blanket, goats, sheep, camels, donkeys, and a bucket. I was given five camels, four females and one male. But they did not do well. These camels were from Somali, they need more water than our Rendille camels. They became weak quickly, they got sick. But they are still alive, although they are not well. I was also given goats and sheep, fifty of them. But many died from the drought. They are beginning to recover.

"I was the worst, poorest person here, so I was given fifty three goats. I was told not to sell them, just eat them and slaughter. But there is a problem here to get money. We go to the traders. We cheat them and ask for credit, 200–300 shillings for two weeks. After two months the traders come looking for us, so we give them a goat to pay for credit. Its a struggle to find money and some people finish off their animals just to buy food.

"Now I am just looking after animals, to water them, to take them back to *fora*, to have children look after them. But I cannot get any more. It is not really sufficient to feed my family. Perhaps if the camels give birth and we have milk, then it will be better for us. I have had these animals for three years now, but they are not very healthy.

"To speak lies is not good in front of God or people. I have told you the truth. The camels have not died. The small stock died just as all Rendille goats died. But it is not true that the animals Nick gives us are bad. That is just something bad that people who are evil say. The only problem is the camels are not growing.

"We are very thankful to Nick because he made us to stay alive up to now. All problems of before, to beg food and milk, now we can rest with our animals, without begging. I have no *shamba* (garden), only these few goats and camels. So I need to save my strength to take these animals to *fora*. If I don't struggle to take care of my animals, I will end up as I did before, with nothing, as Nick found me."[11]

Perhaps more than any other form of assistance, the Ariaal (and Rendille) welcome the restocking of animals, i.e., giving poor families animals for milking and breeding. "Give me two animals, and I can become a rich man," is a common refrain of Ariaal stockowners. Unfortunately, this is one of the least widespread of development assistance offered in the district.

The AIC Mission at Ngurunit

The AIC mission at Ngurunit played an influential role among Ariaal, serving as a rural center that attracted poor Ariaal, similar to the Korr Catholic Mission for Rendille but on a much smaller scale. The Ngurunit mission is situated in a beautiful location at a cut in the Ndoto Mountains that is well watered, forested, and safe from human enemies. Prior to the construction of the mission in 1971, the Ngurunit river provided dry season water for Ariaal cattle, and had several Somali run shops providing outlets for stock sales and grain purchases.

Students at the Adult Literacy Center, Korr, 1990

The AIC missionary who built the Ngurunit mission seemed more comfortable with construction and machinery than with people at the time I first met him in 1974. He viewed Ariaal (as he did the government and the Catholics) as adversaries to be kept at a distance. He opposed Ariaal warriors herding their cattle in the forests above his house, and tried to prevent them from watering their cattle in the water catchment above his house. On one occasion, the missionary squared off with his rifle against spear wielding warriors trying to water their cattle.

He explained his position,

"The Rendille don't have enough sense to see they're killing this area. Two years ago, the water always ran right past the house here—now they've got their cattle up at the water source (a catchment three miles up the canyon) and they're destroying the place. Maybe they don't understand cattle, having just started raising them in addition to camels. But it's going to kill this area. Tell me, why do they keep cattle at all? I know they say 'cattle is wealth', but I just don't understand it. They want large herds that just keep eating, yet their own children are starving. They come to me for *posho*, and I tell them "sell a cow," but no, they won't sell.

"This mountain is supposedly restricted to grazing, but they've got their cattle all over the place. We give them a water hole, and they just keep coming to it. What's the sense of all our work here if there will be no water here later on? Soon this whole mountain will be dust, just like Karare (the large Ariaal village on Marsabit Mountain). Don't they see the damage they're doing? Why don't they have a *baraza'a* (a large public meeting) and discuss how they're using the land? Now they're coming here from Korr, Laisamis, Kulal—all over.

(I asked the missionary if he wasn't encouraging the overgrazing by developing permanent water access?)

"Yeah, the round robin. And they think we're here just to give everything away. It's the Catholics' fault, they just throw food at the Rendille. Only we don't want babies; we want to make men of them."[12]

This missionary rarely visited Ariaal settlements and never raised these issues directly to Ariaal. When I discussed what the missionary had said with Lewogoso elders, Lugi replied,

"It's true that there are more people here now than two years ago. But then Ngurunit was empty. It was *shifta* time when AIC first arrived, and there was nobody here then. But before *shifta*, we always came to this place, there has always been water for our cattle, particularly when its dry. The AIC wanted to build a water tap here, but we didn't want it because it would bring too many Rendille.

"It is true that Rendille are keeping cattle today and didn't use to keep them. But it is not just the cattle that who are drinking the water. Did you see that big tank behind the mission house? That is where the water has gone. Two years the ago wells at Ngurunit were one man deep, sometimes two men. Now they are three men deep, because the water is gone over there.

"The AIC cannot tell us where we can go and where we can't go. We come to this place (Ngurunit) every dry season. Or we search for where the grass is—sometimes Marsabit, sometimes Irrer (on the Milgis River). We cannot have a meeting with all the settlements. Each settlement decides for itself where to go. We go where we can find grass."[13]

The founding AIC missionaries from Ngurunit left Ngurunit in 1978 and were replaced by another American couple, Dale and Suzanne Beverley, who stayed until 1989. Ngurunit had grown a good deal in the 1980s. With funds from InterAid and World Vision, the Beverlys had extended water pipes to several areas of the Ngurunit valley, including the school, dispensary, to livestock troughs, and as taps to individual settlements. In 1990 Ngurunit had over four hundred residents—Ariaal, Rendille, Dorrobo, Samburu and Somali—many of whom had made permanent houses with gardens and fruit trees watered from the new pipes. Ngurunit had become an attractive and viable town.

The Impact of Mission Towns on Ariaal

The activities of the missions have had a large impact on Marsabit District in the past thirty years. Permanent towns now stand where there were previously only water wells, attracting shopkeepers, government workers, and entrepreneurs buying and selling livestock. Many Rendille, Samburu and Ariaal who attended school have become permanent town dwellers, some finding decent employment and housing; others less fortunate search for odd jobs such as cleaning and herding stock to make ends meet. Many town residents have converted to Christianity, some to Islam; many from the pastoral areas come to attend weekly or annual church ceremonies.

Despite the major changes, Ariaal are not opposed to these new influences. Ariaal see the missions as one more resource to utilize in their environment. The new towns are an alternative to rural life, particularly for poor households who have few animals. Furthermore, they are seen as essential centers to gain employment, sell livestock, seek health care, and obtain educations for children.

Said Patrick Ngoley,

"Before we were nomads, we would move with our animals. Now we stay in one place, at Korr or at Kargi. This is *mandeleo* (development). Here we have shops, schools, hospitals. But we still keep our animals in *fora*. When we need money for food we tell our warriors to sell stock at Laisamis, Isiolo, or Merille, They sell them and send us home money. But now everybody is paying for things they used to get for free—meat, transportation, *posho*, milk. People must spend money until rain comes (and animals with milk can return). People must look for work in town making buildings, cleaning houses, even digging urinals. If there is no work, people must sell an animal. If a person is too poor and has no animals or money, he must beg from others."[14]

By and large, it is poorer households with insufficient livestock who are the most likely to move to the towns. The following Figure 5.1 shows the mean livestock ownership of pastoral and settled Ariaal (surveyed at Lewogoso and Ngurunit) and pastoral and settled Rendille (surveyed at Rongumo and Korr).

It is easier to keep animals in the town of Ngurunit than Korr, because it is close to the mountains and has adequate water and grazing. Said a Rendille who had grown wealthy raising camels and trading cattle in Ngurunit,

"Ngurunit is better than Korr. Your camels can stay close to home, you have milk for the family. Grass is never far away, and there is no problem of water. There are insects here, but they are not so bad. You must watch your camels for *zar* (trypanosomiasis), but you can find medicines from UNESCO and the veterinary department."

Although town life implies a non-pastoral (and usually poor) existence, it is in many ways seen as an improvement to rural life. More town-dwelling Ariaal children are enrolled in school than rural children, and more Ariaal adults find wage-paying work from settled communities than from pastoral communities, as illustrated in Figure 5.2.[15]

The larger mission towns, particularly Korr and Kargi, attract more Rendille than Ariaal. I believe this is due primarily to the production system of Ariaal which manages a diversity of livestock types (camels, cattle, and small stock) and which enables the domestic settlement to live with their milk animals close to water and grazing resources. There was not a massive famine relief program among Ariaal as there was among Rendille primarily because the need was much lower among Ariaal.

Figure 5.1. Ariaal Livestock Ownership, Nomadic versus Mission Communities

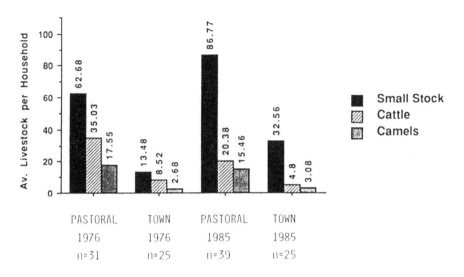

Figure 5.2. Percentage of Ariaal Households with School Children or Wage Workers

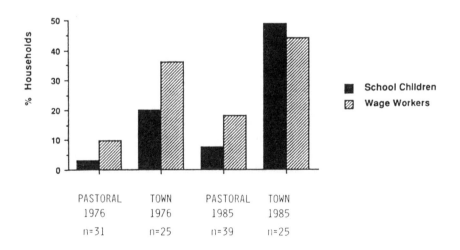

Some Ariaal families move to towns for reasons other than lack of food. My friend Lugi Lengesen moved his senior wife Padamu from Lewogoso to Korr in 1984 while his second wife remained at Lewogoso with three other children to manage his small stock and cattle. Lugi enrolled two of his sons in school and engaged in livestock selling with wages he had earned working for the UNESCO IPAL project.[16]

In 1985 when I visited Korr, Padamu had set her house among other Lukumai Ariaal behind the church. This cluster seemed depressing to me. Houses were covered in plastic or burlap, few had fresh sisal mat covers. There were no animal enclosures as there were no animals, although there was the *na'apu* ritual enclosure in the center of the houses, with its ritual fire constantly lit. Inside Lugi's house Padamu prepared some tea, using donated powdered milk from the mission in place of fresh milk. I asked her how she found life at Korr compared with Lewogoso settlement. I was surprised at her answer:

> "How do I like living here? At Lewogoso, if your child gets sick there is no medicine or help, if you are hungry and there is no food you must walk hours to a shop, and if you need water you must fetch it from the wells at Ngurunit. But here at Korr the shops are close by, there are schools for the children, a dispensary if you get sick. And when I need water, it is right down the hill at the pump. I hope never to return to Lewogoso!"

Padamu's response was an important indication why some Ariaal, like other rural populations, seek to settle in the towns, even though these urban settlements seem impoverished by western standards. Many pastoralists move to the towns not so much in search of famine relief as to seek greater security for their families. Korr and Ngurunit are simply safer and less wearisome places to live than the pastoralist settlements.

Nevertheless, living at the mission settlements creates new problems. Overcrowding and poor sanitation in the mission towns contribute to an increase in infectious diseases and decline in nutrition, especially for those dependent on famine foods.

In 1990 we compared health and nutrition of mothers and under five year olds at three distinct locations—among pastoral Ariaal at Lewogoso Lukumai, among those Rendille settled at Korr Catholic Mission, and among Ariaal and Dorrobo living at Ngurunit. Results showed that where some illness may be higher in the pastoral areas (such as skin infections), hemoglobin levels were significantly lower in children at Korr than among those who kept their animals at Lewogoso and Ngurunit.[17]

Thus in spite of the apparent attractions of town life, Ariaal, for the most part, have not been moved in large numbers to the mission towns. They continue to rely on their animals and live in pastoral settlements close to, but not within, the urban areas. This is an important discovery—given sufficient animals to provide subsistence as well as a surplus to trade, pastoralists see little reason to abandon their well tried economy.

Summary

The missions have had a great impact on Ariaal life, and remain one of the great development influences in the region. Where the northern regions of Kenya were essentially ignored by the colonial government, Catholic and evangelical missions flooded to the area after independence in 1963. The missions built schools, dispensaries, roads, and led to the creation of small towns throughout the region.

Providing food security during periods of drought, mission towns have acted as a magnet to impoverished pastoralists over the past twenty years. They have been the main institution educating pastoralist youth, and most of the educated Rendille and Ariaal are practicing Catholics or Protestants.

The policies of the missions differ. Where the Protestant missions are in general small, concentrating their efforts on water development, Sunday services, and some restocking efforts, the Catholic Church has encouraged wide scale settling of Rendille around their missions, creating urban populations of several thousand people in Korr, Kargi, and Laisamis. The Catholics have not developed alternative food strategies for the former pastoralists, but rather concentrate their efforts on running schools, dispensaries, and church services.

The Ariaal have not settled to a great degree as the Rendille. In part this is because the Catholics concentrated their efforts in the Rendille area while the AIC is more active in the Ariaal areas of Ngurunit and Logologo. But moreover as argued in Chapter 3, the Ariaal have had a more diversified pastoral economy, raising cattle as well as camels and small stock, and do not face famine conditions in the same way as the Rendille.

Of greater consequence to Ariaal life than the missions has been the focused development efforts of the UNESCO-IPAL project, to which we now turn.

Notes

1. Lonsdale 1970:234–237.
2. The Catholic Diocese of Marsabit supervises the missions at Marsabit town, Laisamis, Korr, Kargi, Loiyengalani, Maikona, and North Horr (among others); the missions at Archer's Post, South Horr, Baragoi, and Maralel are supervised in Samburu District.
3. Allen 1981; Republic of Kenya 1984.
4. Markovitz 1973:14 discusses White Father policy in Zaire.
5. See Timberlake 1988:63 for a visitor's impressions of Korr.
6. Interview with K. Esimdehle, Korr. July 11, 1990.
7. Properly speaking, the AIC refers to the church organization in Kenya. Expatriate missionaries are members of the African Inland Mission (AIM), but are commonly referred to as AIC. See Richardson 1968 for official history of the AIC.
8. Tim Ryder, AIC newsletter, Marsabit, June 12, 1990.
9. The AIC built primary schools at Songa, Karare, Logologo and Kijaruni on Marsabit Mountain, and at Gatab (Mt. Kulal) and Ngurunit (Ndoto Mountains), with medical dispensaries at Gatab, Ngurunit, and Logologo (as well as other locations

outside of Marsabit District). The AIC assisted in the development of water projects in Marsabit District (at Karare and Gof Bongole on Marsabit, Gudas near Logologo, Halisuruwa near Korr, and other locations), and agricultural projects on Marsabit Mountain (at Kijaruni, Karare, Nasikakwe, Noduntel, Kulahula and Songa). (Based on interviews with missionaries Herbert Anderson, Dilly Anderson, and Steve Wilson at Logologo.)

10. Interview with Steve Wilson, Logologo, June 18, 1974. The view of "Hamitic" peoples as a lost tribe of Israel is found widely in the writings of 19th century European missionaries in northeastern Africa. See Sutton (1973) for critique of this view.

11. Interview with Halmorkoro Naiyapa, Korr. July 14, 1990.

12. Interview with Charles Barnett, Ngurunit, Nov. 26, 1974.

13. Interview with Lugi Lengesen, Lewogoso, Nov. 26, 1974.

14. Interview with Patrick Surawen Ngoley, July 8, 1990.

15. Roth 1991.

16. See Fratkin 1989a.

17. Nathan and Fratkin 1990.

The UNESCO-IPAL Project

6 In 1974 when I first came to live with the Ariaal, Ngurunit was a small AIC mission center with a few Somali shops, located in a deep cul-de-sac cut into the Ndoto Mountains. The Ariaal of Lewogoso settlement used Ngurunit as a water point for their camels and as their main shopping center for sugar, tea, and grains. When I returned eleven years later, Ngurunit was a larger town with thirty buildings, including an AIC school, a Catholic Church, a dozen shops, a Game Department office, and local offices and storehouses of the UNESCO-IPAL project. About 400 Ariaal, Dorrobo, Rendille, and Somali people lived here full time. Much of the growth of Ngurunit was due to the IPAL project, which had developed a local camp here in 1978, and a permanent structure in the early 1980s.

The Integrated Project in Arid Lands was initiated in Kenya in 1976 by the United Nations as a response to the Sahelian Drought which devastated West African between 1968–1973. Funded by UNESCO's Man and the Biosphere Programme and the United Nations Environment Program (UNEP), IPAL was hailed at the UN Conference on Desertification (held in Nairobi in 1977) as a positive effort to combat environmental degradation by combining scientific research with development programs. As its name implied, IPAL was designed to integrate primary ecological research that monitored desert encroachment with the development of practical techniques to enable local populations to halt further degradation. The predominant view at the Conference on Desertification was that human mismanagement, coupled with rapid population growth of both humans and livestock, had led to the famine in the Sahel region of West Africa in the 1970s.[1]

IPAL's first director was Hugh Lamprey, a wildlife ecologist formerly with the Serengeti Research Institute, who proposed the creation of IPAL stations in northern Kenya, Tunisia, Sudan, and the Mideast. An initial budget of $1,148,200 was designated for the Kenyan project with an additional $1,700,000 for later projects in Tunisia and Sudan. The northern Kenya program was in fact the only IPAL project implemented; by 1985 when the program disbanded, IPAL had spent millions of dollars on primary research, air surveys, road and well-building and marketing projects.[2]

Within its ten year existence, IPAL was transformed from an ecological research project staffed mainly by Europeans and American expatriates, to a major development force staffed by Kenyans with a close working relationship with the District Development Office. IPAL had a profound impact on the economy and life of Marsabit's residents, particularly Ariaal and Rendille, contributing to the growth of the towns built by the missions, increasing the district's trade and commerce, and hiring a substantial number of Rendille and Ariaal as wage workers. IPAL encouraged livestock marketing in the district by developing roads and wells, holding auctions, and visiting pastoral communities with mobile shops to encourage participation in commodity exchange.

Ariaal and Rendille pastoralists were never equal partners in IPAL's projects, however, and their attitudes about IPAL changed from tolerance to high expectations and finally to anger and frustration. A Rendille elder who had worked for IPAL for several years said,

> "UNESCO came with promises, and they left with promises. They promised to help us market our animals, but they ended up buying our animals for nothing and selling them for their own pockets. They flew around in airplanes and attended meetings in foreign countries, but they made us pay for transporting our animals to market. They refused to take our sick children to the hospital, or provide medicines for our camels. So the question is not what UNESCO did for the Rendille, but what did the Rendille do for UNESCO."

From its inception, IPAL saw the reorganization of pastoralist societies as the main way to save the desert ecosystem. "The main longer term objective (of the IPAL plan is) the investigation and development of economic strategies leading to alternative means of livelihood for the nomadic pastoralists," declared an early IPAL proposal.[3] However scientists and planners at IPAL never spelled out what those alternative strategies would be, nor how pastoral populations in arid lands could survive without their animals.

IPAL was never a single project but a heterogeneous assortment of researchers and administrators involved in different activities ranging from pure research to building roads and wells. IPAL went through three phases during its ten year existence—a period of ecological research (1976–1980) conducted exclusively by European researchers on Mt. Kulal, a period of experimental work (1978–1982) carried out by European and African researchers in Ngurunit, Kulal, and Marsabit, and a final period (1982–85) of development activity with IPAL engaged in road-building, well digging, and the creation of livestock auctions and transportation. By 1983 West Germany had taken over most of IPAL's funding, and by 1985 the project ceased to exist independently but was absorbed into various programs of the Kenyan government.

Ecological Research on Mt. Kulal

In 1976, IPAL established a station of prefabricated buildings near the AIC mission at Gatab high on Mt. Kulal in Marsabit District. To most observers, Mt. Kulal (altitude 2293 meters), which is a cold, windy and isolated location, is an unlikely place to "monitor desert encroachment." It is uninhabited by pastoralists (except those settled around the AIC mission at Gatab), and is only utilized by Rendille, Samburu, and Boran for and cattle grazing during severe dry periods. Given IPAL's objectives, it seemed an odd choice of headquarters for a project that intended to examine human interactions with the environment as well as introduce improved management techniques.

Under Lamprey, IPAL avoided interacting with local pastoralists as much as possible. The project's research scientists, nearly all European biologists or ecologists drawn from the Serengeti Research Institute (which studies wild animal interactions in the Serengeti Park in Tanzania), focused their research on measuring vegetation, range productivity, soils and hydrology, and domestic animal production based on observations of livestock confined to paddocks on Kulal. Research on the "human component" of the ecology was confined mainly to aerial surveys photographing domestic herd densities in the large IPAL study area.

IPAL researchers avoided direct interviews or observations with Ariaal or Rendille, who lived in the lowlands distant from Mt. Kulal. They also lived at a colonial-structured distance from their African support staff. European researchers at the Kulal station were given modular homes with one and two bedrooms, solar-heated hot water, private toilets, and standing orders for fruit and vegetables flown in on a regular basis from Nairobi. African staff, in contrast, lived in rows of single-room cubicles, each with one window, a bunk bed, and chair, and sharing a common latrine. The African staff ate separately, mainly *posho*, cabbage, and potatoes driven up by lorry from Nairobi on a four to six-week basis.[4]

IPAL, under Lamprey, never explored how the pastoralists used the land in terms of socio-cultural adaptations of mobility, herd diversity, and kinship networks. Based on their previous work in the Serengeti Game Park where Maasai pastoralists were prohibited from grazing their cattle on park lands (based on long-standing but untested assumptions that pastoral herds competed with wild ungulates), IPAL consistently held the view that Marsabit District's pastoralists were responsible for environmental degradation and dessication in the region.[5] In his proposal to establish IPAL in Marsabit District, director Lamprey wrote,

"Considerably more than half the total land area of Kenya is semi-arid or arid rangeland inhabited by pastoral peoples with their livestock. . . . The rangelands are being increasingly damaged by overstocking and incorrect management regimes. A large part of northern Kenya is irreversibly degraded and the processes of desertification have reached an advanced stage."[6]

IPAL's conclusions were drawn even before the data were collected. IPAL's meticulous (and expensive) aerial photography of the 22,000 km^2 study area in western Marsabit District, provided evidence of overgrazing around Korr, Kargi, and Marsabit Mountain, which was promoted widely in the early IPAL reports. But little attention was paid to the fact that there was very little grazing around Mt. Kulal and Lake Turkana, traditional Rendille herding areas. Any Rendille or Ariaal (if questioned) would have told IPAL researchers that they stayed away from Kulal due to extensive stock raiding by the Turkana, and that they had moved *en masse* to the famine-distribution points at Korr, Kargi, and Laisamis since 1973 to escape drought and political insecurity in the region. But these social and historical factors were not included in IPAL's reports, and "overgrazing" was described as if it were a permanent condition.

IPAL researchers were not interested in looking at the traditional pastoral practices of the Rendille. They conducted studies of livestock production on sample camels and goats and sheep confined to experimental paddocks on Kulal, meticulously recording variations in milk yields, growth and reproductive rates of their sample herds.[7] These measurements do not reflect the conditions of animals managed in the lowlands by the local pastoralists and tell us little about pastoral production or actual land use. Yet Lamprey seriously expected that the results of the IPAL experiments would be used to demonstrate improved techniques in herd management to the pastoralists. It is not surprising that Ariaal and Rendille viewed IPAL with skepticism and indifference.

A Rendille elder remarked,

"You ask me what UNESCO did for us? How do I know what they did? They were like a mirage, we never saw them, we did not know where they stayed, what they did. Sometimes we would see them in the airplanes, or a vehicle driving to Marsabit. They never stopped for us."

Experimental Phase:
The Traditional Livestock Management Project

It was only during its intermediate stage of experimental veterinary work among the pastoral settlements that Ariaal responded enthusiastically to IPAL.

An independent project later affiliated to IPAL, the Traditional Livestock Management Program (TLMP) was initiated in 1978 by the veterinary biologist H.J. Schwartz with funding from the Federal Republic of Germany (FRG). Schwartz and his associates were interested in studying pastoral camel production and making relevant and low cost veterinary improvements in productivity. TLMP built a station in the lowlands at Ngurunit from which the biologists visited Ariaal and Rendille settlements on a regular basis. Focusing on an Ariaal herd of sixty camels owned by Masala settlement, the TLMP over several years investigated feeding habits and the incidence of infectious diseases and parasites. Furthermore, TLMP arranged for consultancy reports on Ariaal and Rendille camel strategies including a history of Rendille movements and a study of trading activities in Korr.[8]

Schwartz and his colleagues began a program of active veterinary care not only for the experimental herds but for various Ariaal settlements in the Ngurunit area. Veterinary medicines were distributed or sold at cost to

Figure 6.1 Mean Growth Rate of Camel Calves in Treated and Non-Treated Herds

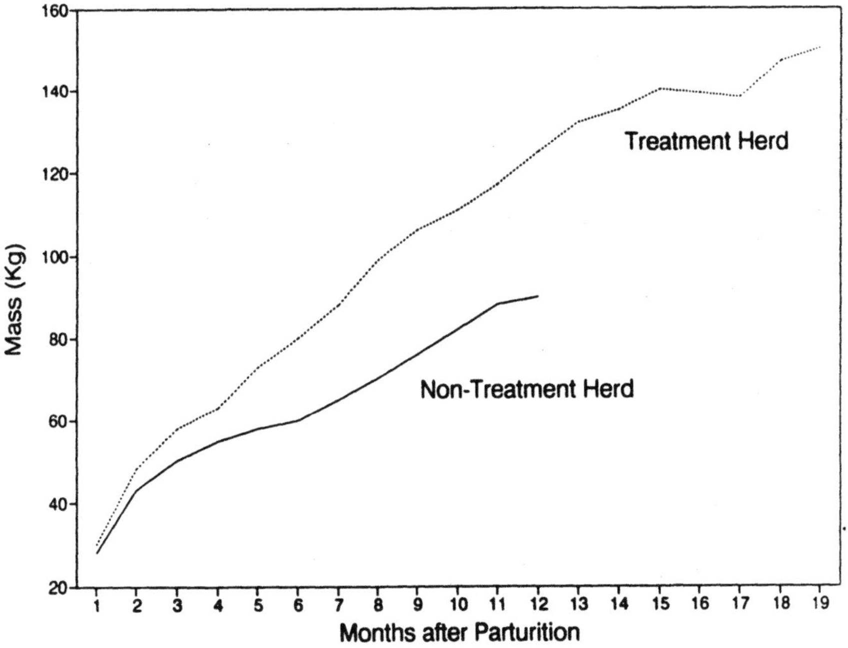

Source: Simpkin 1985:126

treat trypanosomes, ticks, and worms, and veterinary assistance was offered in the delivery of calves and treatment of traumas. Schwartz and his colleagues found that by reducing the enormous worm loads of the camels (particularly *haemonchus* nematodes in the gastrointestinal tract) milk production doubled without incurring any further loss to the existing vegetation, as the vegetation now fed the camels rather than their parasites. The TLMP researchers developed a low cost and accessible treatment program against worms by placing antihelminthic medicines mixed with salt in a half rubber tire placed in the camel enclosures. In this way the camels dosed themselves with the medicine mixture, stopping when they had enough salt.[9] Figure 6.1 compares the mean growth rate of camel calves in treated and untreated herds, and Figure 6.2. compares the mean lactation rate of camel dams in treated and untreated herds in the IPAL study at Ngurunit.

Inspired by his results, Schwartz proposed that IPAL implement a larger version of his program of veterinary care to other settlements throughout the Rendille area. The plan was rejected because, as IPAL directors had declared, "IPAL is a research project and not a development one". IPAL had no interest in improving livestock production, their major concern was to destock the region. The only development work IPAL considered was how to get the pastoralists to sell more animals. At this point, Schwartz quit IPAL, and continued his research independently in Isiolo District. IPAL

<u>Figure 6.2 Mean Lactation Rate for Treated and Non-Treated Camel Dams</u>

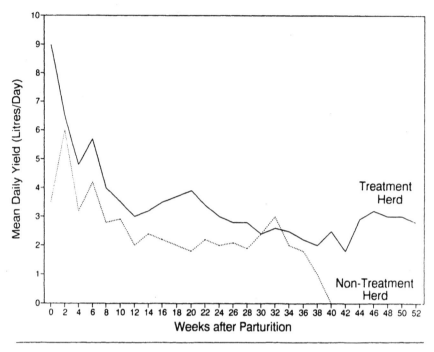

Source: Simpkin 1985:115-116

did not continue Schwartz's work among the lowland settlements, and the TLMP came to a halt.

Ariaal settlements near Ngurunit had come to depend on the TLMP project to supply veterinary assistance and medicines. When the project ended, many Ariaal grew increasingly bitter about UNESCO. As one elder explained it,

"Only Jurgen (Schwartz) and Rutagwenda (Schwartz's associate) were good for us. They gave us medicines for *zar* (trypanosomiasis), they helped us when the camels gave birth. And they charged us nothing for this. They were the only ones who asked 'what do the Rendille need for their camels?' But the others at UNESCO do nothing for us. Now when UNESCO drives through Korr and we say "Please take this child to the hospital (at Marsabit) they say *'Mutum'* ('you cannot have this'). So we think nothing of UNESCO."

IPAL's Development Phase

Marsabit District's political representatives grew increasingly impatient with the IPAL researchers on Kulal. A great deal of money was pouring into the district with very little visible benefit to its inhabitants, and both the Rendille's elected MP (Member of Parliament) and the District Commissioner were voicing their concerns to Nairobi. The Kenyan government had been lobbying UNESCO, as well as other international aid agencies, to increase their staff with Kenyan nationals, not simply to find employment for nationals (as cynics charged) but because, as the government argued, these programs needed to be run by Kenyans for Kenyans.

The Kenya government was also concerned that large international programs focus more on applied development work and not just conduct basic research, to assist in the country's overall development. IPAL's budget was now funded by the European Economic Community and Germany in particular, (UNEP having withdrawn sponsorship earlier for financial reasons). The Germans, sensitive to Nairobi's requests and their own economic interests, agreed to a greater development role for the project.

Lamprey was removed as director and IPAL was reorganized under Dr. W.J. Lusigi, a Kenyan ecologist trained in Germany. Lusigi's interests were in applied as well as primary research, and he had great impact on shaping IPAL's new role. A new headquarters was built in Marsabit town closer to government offices and major transportation routes; Ngurunit was expanded as an IPAL field station and new stations were created at Illaut, Illeret, Marsabit, and Korr. Mt. Kulal continued as the research base for paddock studies and aerial surveys. Most of the educated Kenyans hired for the project however were not local but recruited from central or western Kenya, although local Rendille and Ariaal pastoralists were hired to herd experimental animals and serve as watchmen and cooks.

Lusigi developed a comprehensive development plan that combined both conservation efforts to protect degraded resources with programs designed to improve pastoral production, education, extension services, and livestock marketing. A Kenyan economist who had studied Rendille economy was brought in to develop livestock marketing resources in western Marsabit District, and consultancy reports were undertaken on Rendille and Gabra pastoral ecology, market behavior, education, and extension services.[10]

IPAL became highly visible in the district, with permanent camps, stores, and transportation pools located throughout the district. Local Ariaal and Rendille pastoralists, few of whom had ever worked for wages, were hired to dig wells, herd livestock, and construct buildings.

Despite their increased interaction with the local peoples, IPAL's orientation towards pastoralism remained very similar to Lamprey's view. For both Lamprey and Lusigi, rehabilitation of the vegetation meant getting Ariaal and Rendille cattle off it. Where Lamprey would have preferred massive culling (i.e., forced stock sales or slaughter), or the imposition of grazing restrictions on Ariaal and Rendille cattle herds ("Can't these people see this is not cattle country?," Lamprey once exclaimed), Lusigi focused more practically (and humanely) on inducing the pastoralists to sell their animals. This is the main reason IPAL under Lusigi focused their attention on improving the livestock marketing infrastructure.

Much of IPAL's development plan was aimed at reducing the absolute numbers of animals in the pastoral areas. The plan called for grazing controls ("exclusion zones") to allow rangeland time to recover, and for the establishment of land tenure through the registration of rangeland through title deeds to "tribal groups" (similar to the group ranch idea in Maasailand). The plan also called for improving public security, extending fixed water points, improving the delivery of veterinary and human health care, providing drought assistance, providing banking and credit opportunities, and improving of livestock marketing.[11]

Many of these goals are praiseworthy and necessary to raise pastoral productivity and conserve their natural resources. Improving public security, particularly the ability to graze one's animals without fear of armed raiders, was and is a pressing concern to most of the regions' pastoralists. Other ideas, such as development of bank and credit facilities, are more novel but are nevertheless spreading among pastoralists looking for ways to invest capital safely while insuring against catastrophic losses.

The creation of fixed water points came as a mixed blessing, and in several cases Ariaal and Rendille elders were opposed to it. Mechanizing a well, even with a hand pump, enables more animals to be watered in a shorter time, and leads directly to overgrazing areas that previously could support large animal populations. The Ariaal settlement of Lewogoso was one of only a few settlements that used the Milgis flood waters near Baiyo mountain; they feared a mechanical pump would attract other settlements and cause their animals to suffer. IPAL was aware of this fact, which was spelled out in a consultancy report by historian Neal Sobania who described migration and settlement patterns of the regions pastoralists, but like many other consultancies, this was ignored by IPAL.[12]

Most of the IPAL proposals, however, were never implemented (e.g., the creation of "exclusion zones," banking services, or improving police security), others were only partially established (the improvement of water resources and development of water resources). IPAL's greatest success was in the area of livestock marketing, an endeavor supported strongly by those area entrepreneurs most likely to benefit from its development, including the county council officials, large traders, and government employees making some money on the side. Not surprisingly, certain IPAL personnel themselves benefited from the increased livestock trade in the area.

The Western Marsabit
Integrated Development Pilot Project (WMIDPP)

IPAL concentrated much of its financial and labor resources in livestock marketing. This came about mainly through the initiative and energy of their livestock marketing director George Njiru, who proposed the creation of the Western Marsabit Integrated Development Pilot Project (WMIDPP), an unwieldy name referred to simply by Ariaal as "UNESCO". The main idea behind WMIDPP was to increase market integration of the Ariaal and Rendille by encouraging their taste for (and thereby their increased demand for) commodity goods (e.g., cloth, tea, sugar), which in turn would lead to an increased sale of small stock and cattle to obtain cash to purchase more goods.

Njiru reasoned that the Rendille would sell more livestock not only if marketing structures (roads, auctions, and credit institutions) improved, but if the pastoralists had greater incentive to sell their animals. With considerable ingenuity, Njiru organized mobile shops on camel-back which carried tea, sugar, grain, tobacco, cloth, shoes and cooking pots from village to village.

Njiru was frank about WMIDPP's purpose. In IPAL's Resource Management Plan, its major document, he raised concern that improvements in veterinary care and range resources would lead to large increases in herd size, and thus further hurt the range with overgrazing. IPAL needed to think about ways to attain even higher levels of livestock offtake to prevent this greater degradation. "Failing this," Njiru wrote, "such improvements will lead to an acceleration of the trend towards deterioration which is already evident around trading centers." He argued that promoting livestock sales would relieve pressures on the land, improve the pastoralists standard of living, integrate the area into the national economy, and get meat protein into other areas of Kenya.[13]

The WMIDPP plan fell in nicely with government development interests which had long wanted to increase beef trade from the pastoral regions to the cities.[14] IPAL's WMIDPP offered the best opportunity to achieve this, particularly as IPAL and West Germany were footing the bill.

Njiru proposed developments in marketing infrastructure; he administered IPAL projects in water development, the mobile shops, and arranged for administration road crews to smooth tracks between the pastoralist communities. Most importantly, Njiru developed livestock auctions begun at Illaut and Korr to buy both small stock and cattle. WMIDPP held their auctions monthly and provided transportation for the animals directly to the markets (and higher prices) at Nanyuki and Nairobi.

From the outset, IPAL's auctions were unpopular with both the pastoralists and the local traders, particularly the Somali shopkeepers whose own trade in livestock was being undermined. Ariaal complained that the prices paid for cattle at the auctions were too low, a feature compounded by the fact that IPAL were often the only bidders. Shopkeepers who had bought and traded small stock in exchange for credits to the pastoralists, complained that IPAL could offer better prices because IPAL had subsidized transportation (the trucks, fuel, and drivers lodging being paid by UNESCO), while the shopkeepers had to bear these costs themselves.[15] Both the Ariaal and Somalis distrusted the IPAL traders (most of whom were "down-country" Kikuyu or other groups from central Kenya) and suspected that IPAL staff were profiting personally from the livestock sales. In time, Ariaal and Rendille stopped selling at the auctions, reverting back to their older method of trading livestock to shopkeepers in exchange for credit.

Local Ariaal employed by WMIDPP also resented their working relationship with IPAL, complaining of low pay and poor working conditions. An Ariaal elder once asked,

"Tell me, if I was to spear UNESCO, would there be a court of law that would find me guilty? They offered us wages to dig a well near our village, twenty five shillings a day each for four men. They told us we could find water there, and if we dug the well, they would provide a hand pump. So for three days we dug this well. When we could not find water, UNESCO said it was our fault and they would not pay us what they promised. Surely I should spear this man."

Ironically one of the most visible benefits of the IPAL project *was* the employment of local pastoralists for cash wages. Several dozen Ariaal and Rendille elders in the Ngurunit and Korr areas held jobs ranging from security and herding to construction and driving. Stockowners who had lost quite a few animals during the 1982 drought were able to recover quickly by investing their wages in small stock and rebuilding their herds. Lugi Lengesen, who had less than thirty goats and a few cattle in my 1976 census, had by 1985 attained a sizable herd of thirty cattle and one hundred small stock. Much of this wealth was based on transactions he had made from his wages as a watchman in the Ngurunit camp for three years.

Dr. Lusigi commented,

"We thought that paying local people wages for UNESCO work would encourage them to buy goods from the shops and sell their livestock. It had the opposite effect. We did a small survey at Ngurunit and found that the men who worked for us were getting good wages, many for the first time in their lives. Invariably they invested most of it in livestock. So what we were trying to accomplish— to get the Rendille to sell more animals—did not work."

It is remarkable that despite years of research in the area, IPAL staff were surprised that their Ariaal and Rendille workers were converting their wages into livestock. IPAL had not yet grasped (and in fact never did understand) the importance of livestock to the people of this area, that animals are not only the basis of survival, but the medium of social relations that holds pastoralist society together. Furthermore, their survey revealed a little appreciated fact about pastoralists—not only do they sell livestock, but they are active buyers as well. In a 1982 study of Samburu stock sales by members of a group ranch, the majority of cattle sales were of older or infirm steers, the payment for which was used to buy young steers and heifers. Sales were made to rejuvenate the herd, not to accumulate cash.[16]

This points to a critical difference in the reasons why Ariaal and other subsistence pastoralists sell animals versus those of commercial entrepreneurs, and why in fact the WMIDPP project ultimately failed.

Livestock Marketing Among Ariaal

Ariaal and Rendille are largely subsistence pastoralists, producing animals for milk and meat and exchanging surplus animals for both ritual and economic purposes. But Rendille pastoralists have sold or traded surplus livestock since at least the 19th century to Somali, Swahili, or Ethiopian

Table 6.1 Average Livestock Transactions per Lewogoso Household [19]

	1976	1985
Camels owned	14.4	16.7
Camels sold	0	0
Cattle owned	31.5	22.0
Cattle sold (%)	3.6 (11%)	1.7 (7%)
Small stock owned	68.8	88.6
Small stock sold	10.9 (15%)	4.0 (4%)
Annual cash income (K.Sh.)	1172.50($98)	2445($150)

traders.[17] IPAL's data shows that in 1980 Rendille sold 5.2% of their cattle, 0% camels, and 7.6% of their small stock to local traders.[18] Figures from my research among Ariaal households in 1976 are even higher; as shown on Table 6.1, Ariaal at Lewogoso sold 11% of their cattle and 15% of their small stock to local shopkeepers. In 1985 these same households reduced the number of animals sold to recover from the drought, selling only 7% of their cattle and 4% small stock. Nevertheless, Ariaal livestock sales in 1985 provided households with an average household income of $150.00 in both periods.[19]

Ariaal sell livestock primarily to purchase other foods. Seventy percent of Ariaal income is spent on cereals, sugar, tea, and tobacco, and the remainder is used to pay for household goods, taxes, school fees, and livestock purchases.[20]

Wealthier households purchased considerably more non-food commodities (cloth, utensils, additional livestock) than poor households, who spent more of their income on food purchases. In a study of thirty Rendille households, IPAL researcher Michael O'Leary found that wealthy households generated 60% more cash income than poorer households but spent relatively less (38%) for cereals than poor households (46% of their expenditure), as shown on Table 6.2. Poor pastoralists are in a double bind. They must sell more animals for food than wealthy households, yet by having fewer animals they become increasingly impoverished, particularly if an extended drought wipes out their stock holdings necessary to purchase foods. Both the Ariaal and Rendille sell considerably more animals during the dry season than the wet, and more stock are sold during drought years than non-drought years when milk supplies are low and the need to purchase grains increases. Unfortunately, this is also the time when the market is flooded with animals in poor condition and meat prices are at their lowest.

Livestock Marketing in Marsabit District

Livestock marketing in Marsabit District is not as well regulated as in other parts of the country, and the government takes a non-interventive role. Pastoralists sell surplus stock (usually older male animals) to small

Table 6.2 Consumption Patterns among Rendille

		POOR	RICH
INCOME			
	wages	149	208
	gifts	99	132
	livestock products	619 (71%)	1061 (75%)
	TOTAL	867 K.Sh.	1401 K.Sh.
EXPENSES			
	cereals	406 (40%)	544 (35%)
	sugar	156 (15%)	277 (18%)
	tea	79 (8%)	126 (8%)
	clothes	78 (8%)	122 (8%)
	footwear	28 (3%)	44 (3%)
	jewelry	11 (1%)	38 (2%)
	tobacco	77 (8%)	108 (7%)
	gifts	48 (5%)	67 (4%)
	misc.	127 (13%)	227 (15%)
	TOTAL	1010 (100%)	1553 (100%)

Source: O'Leary 1985:125

local traders, often Somali shopkeepers who have lived in the region for generations. The shopkeepers offer credit to pastoral households, collecting their debt once or twice a year when they can transport the animals down country or to larger buyers. Pastoralists generally sell their livestock in the dry season when milk supplies are low and they need supplemental grain and sugar calories. (Figure 6.3 shows seasonal variation in small stock sales in Korr.) Unfortunately this is also the time when the animal's condition is poorest and prices at their lowest. If the small trader can hold the animals while they fatten during the rainy season, he will receive a higher price. It is not unusual for traders to hire pastoral herders to tend these animals until they drive them to market by foot or in a vehicle.

Shopkeepers and pastoralist entrepreneurs will usually sell stock to a middleman who transports the animals to market, or else rent space on the truck themselves and try to sell their livestock at the more profitable markets in Isiolo, Nanyuki, or Nairobi. A male goat which would fetch 160 shillings ($10.00) in Illaut or Ngurunit would fetch twice that amount in Isiolo, less the transport fee of 30–45 shillings ($2.00–3.00). However, transporting livestock south entails higher risks including dehydration and death en route; the government forbids sale of these dead animals (although carcasses can be sold illegally to local butchers for low prices). Sellers also face the risk that they may not be able to sell their animals at a good price for some time, and will incur additional expenses waiting for a sale.

The development of livestock services to the pastoral regions is impeded by the government's concentration of resources in the private ranches in the south. While government veterinary services and commercial credit are readily available to the private ranchers of Laikipiak or Narok Districts,

Figure 6.3. Seasonal Variation in Small Stock Sales at Korr

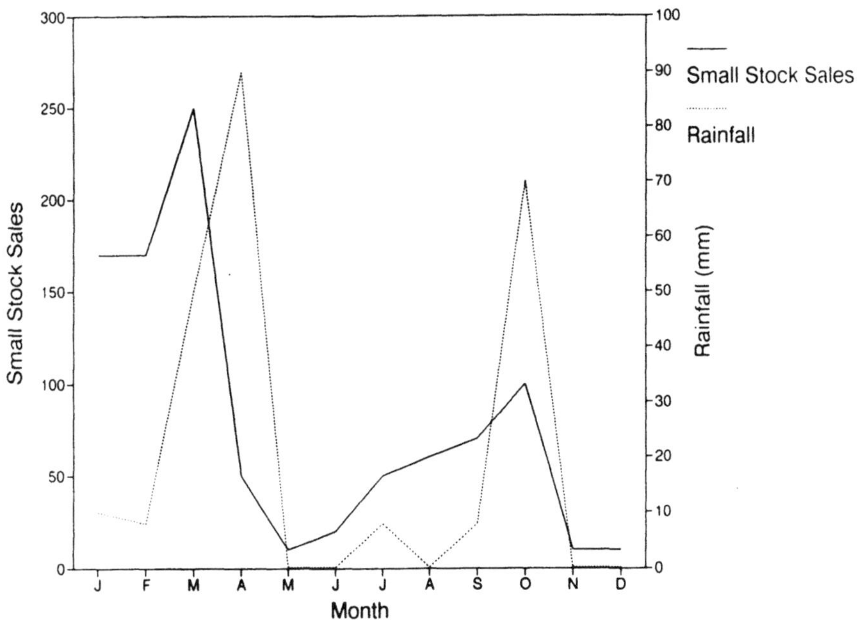

Source: Schwartz and Schwartz 1985: 14

they are rare, infrequent, or absent in areas of subsistence pastoralism to the north and south. The Livestock Marketing Division (LMD) organizes auctions and veterinary services and its affiliate, the Kenya Meat Commission (KMC), buys and sells beef to domestic and international consumers. However, there are no KMC facilities in Marsabit, and the LMD only buys cattle in Marsabit at auctions held once or twice a year, at irregular times and announced only a few weeks in advance. It was intended that the WMIDPP would address this problem, but their auctions were generally unattended by larger buyers to the south.[21]

There has been some improvement in the delivery of livestock development services under the present government of President Moi. Since 1978 local veterinary officers in Marsabit town have provided inoculations and medical treatment against trypanosomiasis, but these services are rare or inaccessible for the pastoral settlements below Marsabit Mountain. In part this is due to lack of funds, since veterinary officers have few vehicles or an inadequate budget for petrol to visit the pastoral communities regularly, but it also reflects an inertia and lack of commitment by the government to rural pastoral areas.

Furthermore, the delivery of government livestock services throughout the country is hopelessly entangled in government bureaucracy which allocates specific responsibilities to different departments and even whole ministries, leading to competition between the various departments for resources in vehicles, fuel, salaries, and housing.

For example, the Ministry of Livestock Development (MLD) is responsible for veterinary services, range management, animal production, and marketing, but in Marsabit their activities are limited to periodic sales of veterinary medicines and veterinary examinations of beef butchered in the towns. If people seek to form associations, as did women in Marsabit organizing a cooperative to sell milk in town, they must seek licensing from the Ministry of Cooperative Development; to obtain loans and credit they must apply to Kenya Commercial Bank (under the Ministry of Finance). To seek animals through restocking one applies to the Ministry of Culture and Social Services; to find training in veterinary skills the Ministry of Agriculture; yet adult literacy is administered through the Ministry of Education. Land use for grazing rights may fall under the Ministry of Tourism and Wildlife if using national parks or reserves, but may be challenged by the newly created Ministry of Reclamation of Arid and Semi-Arid Lands, who are responsible for stocking rates and land use in northern Kenya.

These bureaucratic divisions and ensuing rivalries impede further development efforts. A major project aimed at improving camel productivity in Marsabit District was proposed by the German Development Corporation (GTZ) in 1988 as a follow up to IPAL's Traditional Livestock Management Project, with biologist Jurgen Schwartz as a consultant. This project intended to provide services to pastoralist communities, including restocking, introducing improved bulls for husbandry, and providing low-cost veterinary care and medicines, including treatments for trypanosomiasis, ticks and worms.

The GTZ project was delayed implementation due to competition between two governmental agencies for its sponsorship (and copious funds)—the Kenya Agricultural Research Institute (KARI) of the Ministry of Agriculture, and the Department of Range Management of the Ministry of Livestock Development. The project finally was won by Range Management, who used much of the first year's budget to fund administrative offices, personnel salaries, and new vehicles in Nairobi. By 1990 the government was debating whether to headquarter the GTZ project in Marsabit or Korr, where Range Management favored the district capital with its superior roads and amenities, and the GTZ staff wishing to locate at Korr where the Rendille and their camels lived. The who had been told of new coming veterinary services for a long time, resigned themselves to an attitude of "we'll believe it when we see it."

The failure of the camel extension program followed directly upon the collapse of the UNESCO-IPAL project. Both were built on mountains of promises, with agents telling Ariaal and Rendille stockowners of the wonderful new services that would soon benefit them. But the agencies coming into Marsabit District in the past fifteen years have left little to the Ariaal and Rendille except bitterness and skepticism about governmental projects in general.

By 1983 the role of UNESCO in IPAL had declined, and the project developed into the Kenya Arid Lands Research Station (KALRES) funded by the German government.[22] Njiru's WMIDPP was taken over for a time by the Kenya Agricultural Research Institute (KARI), but it never assumed the active role it had under Njiru.

UNESCO-IPAL's Effect on Ariaal

IPAL's primary goal was to study and reduce environmental degradation in arid regions. Attached to this was their stated intention to promote improved techniques in land and resource management for the pastoral peoples living in these regions. However IPAL avoided studying or developing improvements in livestock production, but instead focused their attention and considerable resources on improving livestock marketing as the principle means to conserve the range.

Schwartz's research in the TLMP showed that low-cost veterinary intervention could increase camel milk production and conserve existing vegetation. Yet it was rejected by IPAL who feared that the pastoralists' tendency to "maximize their herds" would lead to further overgrazing and environmental deterioration. IPAL consistently held this view of "pastoral irrationality" despite a large number of reports (by both independent researchers and their own consultants) which showed that pastoral herd growth was limited by periodic drought, disease, and by the pastoralists' own constraints on labor.[23] IPAL leadership held to their views and consistently chose to improve marketing conditions rather than improve veterinary care or training.

IPAL intended to integrate Ariaal and Rendille into the cash market by increasing demand for store-bought goods (through increasing the pastoralist's access to goods via the mobile shops) in order to increase the supply of livestock to the market (via the new auctions, water points, and growing towns). UNESCO-IPAL had a large effect on Ariaal because they were the principal target of IPAL's experimental projects in veterinary care (Schwartz's TLMP) as well as the target population for Njiru's WMIDPP marketing improvements. The WMIDPP employed Ariaal men to help dig wells, build enclosures, herd animals, and transport goods in the mobile shops, and IPAL provided Ariaal herds with veterinary care and services (at least during Schwartz's TLMP etween 1978–1982). Because much of IPAL's developmental work was based in Ngurunit, Ariaal had easier access to sell and buy livestock, purchase necessary goods and food, and earn wages from IPAL.

Figure 6.4 shows the increase in wage labor for Ariaal and Rendille between 1976 and 1985, measured in surveys from Lewogoso settlement and Rendille settlements around Korr. Most employment opportunities were found with Schwartz's Traditional Livestock Management Project (TLMP) or Njiru's West Marsabit Integrated Development Pilot Project (WMIDPP).

Although Ariaal were earning wages and buying household goods, they did not increase their sales of livestock. In 1975 Ariaal sold 7% of their cattle and 15% of their small stock; in 1985 they sold only 4% of their

Figure 6.4 Wage Labor in Ariaal and Rendille, 1976 and 1985

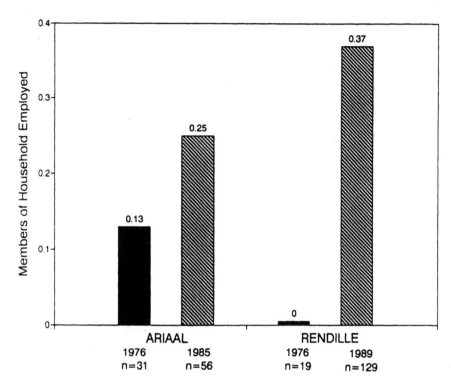

cattle and 11% of their small stock. Figure 6.5 compares livestock sales among Ariaal and Rendille, and shows the decline in Ariaal sales following the 1982–1984 drought, but the increase in Rendille sales, particularly of cattle. This reflects the increasing integration of Rendille in the livestock marketing brought about by both IPAL's livestock auctions and the increase in cattle ownership among the Rendille. Where IPAL attempted to reduce cattle herd size in Marsabit District, they in fact increase cattle herd size as cattle became an important commodity for market exchange.

Livestock sales declined in 1985 mainly because this was a post-drought recovery period in which Ariaal concentrated on building up their herds, selling old and infirm animals and buying young stock, particularly cattle. While market integration increased, Ariaal livestock transactions were aimed at building up their herds rather than reducing them.

Ariaal behavior in the marketplace was quite different than that expected by IPAL, who thought the Ariaal and Rendille would sell more animals to purchase the newly available shop goods. The fact that Ariaal did not increase their livestock sales points to a fundamental difference between the economy of livestock pastoralism practiced by the Ariaal and that of commercial livestock production, promoted by IPAL and their allies in the Ministry of Livestock Development.

Figure 6.5 Livestock Sales among Ariaal and Rendille

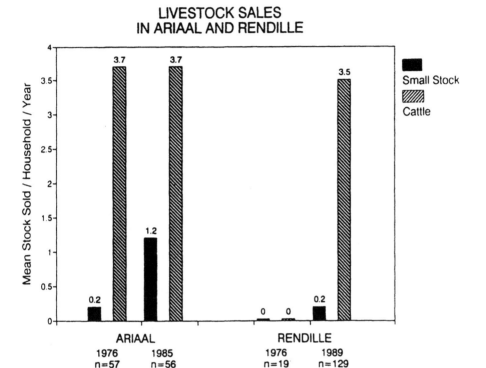

LIVESTOCK SALES
IN ARIAAL AND RENDILLE

Ariaal pastoralism is an economy where livestock are raised is to produce a steady and regular supply of food for their human herders. Female animals, particularly camels, are raised for milk, small stock for meat and exchange for grains (particularly as the dry season progresses), and cattle are kept for bridewealth and ritual consumption. Commercial production such as ranching, on the other hand, is an economy which concentrates on the production of young male steers for sale, where animals are sold young while their meat is tender and the investment costs are low.

Expansion into the commercial market is not in itself a bad thing, and many pastoralists welcome the prospect of obtaining better prices, improved veterinary care, and cheaper transport of their stock to market as promised by IPAL. The problem in Marsabit District was that IPAL and the Ministry of Livestock Development used the model of private commercial ranch production as the form this marketing should take. Throughout the pastoral regions of Kenya, the government made efforts to privatize communal lands into group or individual plots, a move that benefits a few entrepreneurs at the expense of the majority of subsistence pastoralists.

UNESCO-IPAL never attempted to work as partners with the Ariaal or Rendille. As with the missionaries, Ariaal were objects to be changed, to be developed, to be saved. It was as if these people had no purpose or vision of their own that was worth knowing or understanding.

Rendille and Ariaal understand this paternalistic attitude quite well. A leading Rendille elder was asked what he thought the Rendille's future would be with all these developments, and he replied,

> "Every foreigner who came here—the missionaries, UNESCO—all came with their own ideas of what was right for the Rendille. Now you come to me and ask what is our future. It's a bit backwards, isn't it? Why didn't you ask us at first before deciding what was good for the Rendille? That's all I have to say of it."

Like the missionaries, IPAL viewed the pastoralists as irrational, childish, ignorant. By the time Lusigi had replaced Hugh Lamprey as director of IPAL, the project was already unpopular among the Rendille. One of the first tasks of the reorganized IPAL was to hold a large meeting among Rendille at Korr, a meeting attended by the District Commissioner (DC) and local District Officers (DOs) to encourage more cooperation from the Rendille. A Rendille elder, in describing the meeting, said,

> "We heard from the DO that UNESCO said our cattle were destroying the trees, but how can cattle destroy trees? When it is dry we need to take our cattle into the mountains, but when it is green (wet) we bring them here to Korr. It is true there is not enough grass for our animals here at Korr because there are too many people here, so we take our animals to *fora*. UNESCO accused us of throwing stones at their trucks, but I never saw such a thing. They tell those stories because we are not happy about UNESCO. Those trucks drive too fast anyway, and they *should* be stoned before they run over some child, but we have never done such a thing.
>
> "Those UNESCO people, they may know how to grow gardens down south. But this desert is our garden, and cattle are our fruit. We know how to live here. If UNESCO wants to help, they should give us veterinary medicines, they should train us in how to use the medicines and prevent our animals from dying. That is what they should do."

Notes

1. UNEP 1977. The Sahel (from the word *sahil*, Arabic for "coast" or "shore") is the region south of the Sahara Desert and includes Mauritania, Senegal, Mali, Burkina Faso, Niger, Chad, northern Nigeria, northern Benin, and western Sudan.

2. IPAL 1984; Lamprey 1976; Timberlake 1988.

3. IPAL 1976:4.

4. Neal Sobania, personal communication, March 1990.

5. Ecologist David Western has demonstrated the long standing symbiotic relation between domestic Maasai cattle herds and wild ungulate populations in Amboseli Game Park, and has argued extensively that pastoralists be permitted grazing access to these resources (Western 1982; Western and Finch 1986). Richard Leakey, the new director of Kenyan wildlife conservation efforts, apparently agrees, and has opened the Amboseli and Mara Masai Game parks to controlled Maasai grazing.

6. Lamprey 1976:7–8.

7. See for example Field 1979.

8. Sobania 1980b; Schwartz 1980b.

9. IPAL 1985; Schwartz 1979, 1980b; Rutagwenda 1985.

10. O'Leary 1985; Njiru 1984; IPAL 1985

11. IPAL 1984:484–498.

12. Sobania 1979.

13. IPAL 1984:385, 377–424.

14. See for example the Marsabit District Development Plans, 1984–1988; 1988–1992 (Republic of Kenya 1984a; 1988)

15. Tonah 1988:63–64.

16. Perlov 1983.

17. Dahl 1979b:192–95; Sobania 1980a:293.

18. IPAL 1984:387.

19. 52 households in 1976 and 60 households in 1986 were surveyed. Average price of small stock was 25/= (Kenya shillings) in 1976 and 150/= in 1985; average ox was 250/= in 1976 and 1085/= in 1985. One Kenyan shilling equaled .08 US$ in 1976 and 0.04 US$ in 1985.

20. It can be argued that tea and tobacco are "foods" because they are stimulants and hunger suppressants. They are also consumed more in the dry season than the wet season when milk is plentiful.

21. Tonah 1988:53; IPAL 1984:390.

22. KALRES 1985:4.

23. See for example the IPAL consultancy reports of O'Leary 1985; Schwartz 1979; and Sobania 1979.

Development and Pastoral Production in Kenya

7 Let us step back a moment from the specific situation of the Ariaal and place them in the larger context of livestock development in Kenya. In particular, let us compare the experiences of the Ariaal to those of the Maasai, Turkana, and Rendille, pastoralist groups who face very different problems but whose situations may shed light on the future of Ariaal pastoral development.

As mentioned earlier, pastoralist populations of Kenya include the Maasai (pop. 225,00 in Kenya and 125,00 in Tanzania), Samburu (70,000), Turkana (248,000), Somali (250,000), Rendille (15,000), Ariaal (7000), Boran (30,000) and Gabra (23,000). Although these populations are spread over much of Kenya's arid lands, they make up less than one million of Kenya's 24 million population, the majority of whom are peasant agriculturalists or wage-workers. (Map 7.1 shows the location of Kenya's pastoralist populations).

The development of pastoral regions in Kenya has followed different courses for different areas, reflecting specific ecological and historical conditions. However, most Kenyan pastoralists share mutual problems of restrictions on their grazing lands, increased sedentarization, rural poverty, and the search for alternative livelihoods including farming and seeking wage labor in towns.

Those remaining in the pastoral economy find themselves players in the much larger sphere of the commodity market, and are caught between the pulls of subsistence pastoralism to feed their households, and market production to growing and sell male animals for beef.

Maasai

Few African societies have been as romanticized and popularized by Europeans and Americans, while simultaneously neglected and underdeveloped, as the Maasai. Despite their image as "free and noble warriors," the Maasai have seen their grazing lands continuously reduced by colonial appropriation, the creation of national game parks, the steady incursions of agriculturalists, and most recently by the creation of private titles to individual and "group" ranches which are dividing the remaining land.

Map 7.1 Ethnic Groups of Kenya

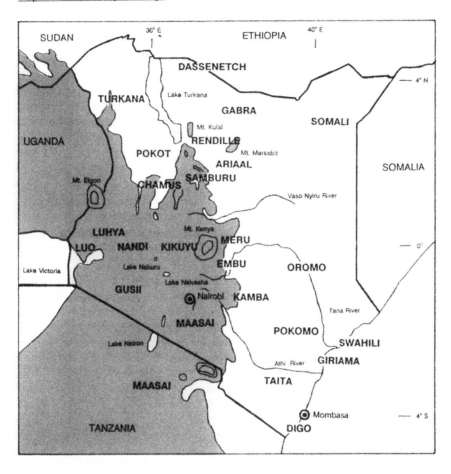

The Maasai are a population of over 350,000 residing in Kenya and Tanzania; their language is shared by another 300,000 people including the Samburu, Chamus, and Ariaal in Kenya and the Arusha and Paraguyu in Tanzania. Never a single political entity, the Maasai are composed of a dozen independent groups including the Kisongo of Tanzania (75,000) and Purko (65,000) of Kenya, as well as the smaller Loita, Matapata, Kaputei, Sikiari, Loitokitok, Damat, Keekonyukie, ilKankeri, and Lo'odokilani Maasai.[1]

In the 19th century Maasailand stretched in an hour-glass shape from the highlands of the central Rift Valley north of Lake Naivasha in central Kenya to the Maasai Steppes of northern Tanzania, encompassing dry plains to the east, wooded savanna and plateaus to the west, and the great lakes of the Kenyan Rift. However by 1900, the boundary between German Tanganiyka and British Kenya cut directly through Maasai lands, and the colonial treaties of 1911 and 1912 pushed the Kenyan Maasai off the central highlands and plains north of the Uganda-Mombassa railroad onto a single reserve in southern Kenya, later administered as Kajiado and Narok Districts.[2]

The British colonial government had taken the most important Maasai dry-season water and grazings lands—the Ngong Hills, Lakes Naivasha and Nakuru, the Mau escarpment in Kenya, and the highland reserves of Mts. Kilamanjaro and Meru in Tanganiyka (now British following Germany's defeat in 1918), which were given over to agricultural production. Furthermore the Maasai were restricted from grazing their livestock near the European estates (for fear of contaminating the European herds) and selling their livestock on the European dominated market, as described earlier.

Confined to 35,000 km² in Kenya and 60,000 km² in Tanzania (60% of their pre-colonial range), the Maasai were further restricted from grazing their cattle in the large game reserves and parks by the National Park Ordinance of 1945 which created Nairobi National Park, Amboseli Reserve, Tsavo West and Mara Masai. Government prohibitions arose from concern that the domestic herds were responsible for degradation to savanna lands, threatening the wildlife of giraffe, wildebeest, and elephants important to tourism revenues and settler recreation.[3]

In addition to grazing restrictions, the Maasai faced competition for land by both expanding agriculturalists and commercial enterprises creating grain and dairy estates. The 1950's was a period of unparalleled growth in human and livestock populations throughout Kenya, brought about by above average rainfall as well as improvements in human health care, rangeland conservation, agricultural production, and veterinary services. Kajiado District's population grew from 22,000 in 1948 to 86,000 in 1969, and to 149,000 in 1979, an average 3.5% growth annually. While some of this growth reflects increasing reproductive rates, Kajiado and Narok Districts grew primarily as Kikuyu and Kamba agriculturalists migrated onto Maasai lands to escape the overcrowding of the central highlands. In 1962 the Maasai constituted 78% of Kajiado District's population; in 1979 they were less than 63%, yielding mostly to Kikuyu and Kamba immigrants.[4]

The majority of people migrating to Maasailand have been poor farmers driven off their lands by large farmers and foreign owned estates. Their situation is hardly improved in Maasailand, as the land is dry and only marginally productive for agriculture except in a few choice areas.

Not all immigrant farmers into Maasailand have been poor, however. Since Independence in 1963, there have been substantial increases in large-scale commercial enterprises taking over Maasai lands. In Narok District, 320,000 hectares of land have been sold to land speculators and farmers since 1980, where the rich and arable land of the Mau Escarpment is now producing commercial wheat and barley.[5] Much of this land has been leased, rented, or sold outright by Maasai owners, who can no longer graze their animals on their former lands.

The ability of Maasai to transfer land individually is a recent phenomenon brought about when the Kenyan government encouraged citizens to title their own land in the 1960s. In traditional Maasai society, no Maasai "owned" grazing or water resources, (although livestock was definitely owned by individuals). Rather land was shared by all members of the *olosho* (territorial section). Following Independence the Kenyan government began to allocate individual sections of land (usually that with the best pasture and permanent water) to progressive (i.e pro-government) Maasai including school teachers, livestock entrepreneurs, shopkeepers, and government officials. It was felt by the government that individual ranches would better contribute to the national livestock market than communal pastoralism, and would set an example for other Maasai. Indeed, these individual Maasai landowners and ranchers became the new "big men" (*ilaiguanani kitok*) in Maasai society.[6]

When, during drought, poor Maasai herded their animals on the better resources of the private ranches (often owned by relatives who could hardly refuse them entry), it became apparent that individual ranches could never accommodate all the Maasai. Resources were simply too thin and patchy throughout Maasailand to subdivide into individual plots. Subsequently in 1968 Kenya passed the Groups Representatives Act which established "grazing blocks" (similar to the colonial "tribal grazing areas" among northern pastoralists) which conferred formal and legal tenure on a community of co-residents, forming the so-called "group ranches."

The pastoral Maasai of Kajiado District in general accepted the group ranch concept as a way to prevent continuing agricultural encroachment on their land and to acquire legal tenure enabling them to qualify for loans and the development of boreholes and cattle dips. However, the government attempted to use the group ranches as a means to control herd size in their larger conservation efforts (aimed mainly at promoting the tourist game parks), and limits were placed on group ranch herd size to qualify for veterinary services and borehole drilling. This met with resistance from poorer Maasai attempting to build up their herds, and in general herd size could not be restricted by government efforts.[7]

Land adjudication has been a mixed blessing for the Maasai. It has conferred land tenure on individuals and local groups and helped prevent agricultural encroachment. Furthermore, as Clare Oxby points out, group ranches have led to an increase in permanent settlement of the elderly and small children, and have increased access to markets and social services including schools and health clinics.[8] Adjudication has not however led to economic security, for ranch boundaries cannot guarantee rain and entire communities have occasionally abandoned their group ranches in search of better pastures, as during the 1968–1973 droughts.

Conceived in large part to increased participation in the commercial livestock market, group ranches have not in themselves led to increased livestock sales. Although the Kenya Meat Commission runs a large meat-packing plant at Athi River in Kajiado District (constructed in the 1930's as a private concern to attract both European and Maasai cattle), livestock marketing in Kajiado has been monopolized by non-Maasai entrepreneurs and a few wealthy Maasai ranchers who, unlike poor subsistence pastoralists, have access to transportation, feeding lots, and appropriate veterinary care. Furthermore, prices on meat in Kenya are often kept artificially low by the central government, leaving the pastoralist little choice but to hold on to his stock for herd reproduction or domestic consumption.

One often hears government agents blaming the Maasai for their "conservatism," holding the former colonial administration's view that pastoralists are reluctant to sell animals due to religious or irrational attachments to their cattle. Yet As Maasai researcher Alan Jacobs notes, it was the British who restricted the Maasai from purchasing, moving, or selling their stock in the first place, and the myth of pastoral conservatism was in large part a British construct used to justify the establishment and maintenance of a European dominated livestock economy.[9]

Today it is not so much cattle that are being monopolized, but as John Galaty notes, *land* that has become the most important resource in Maasailand.[10] The process of privatizing land in individual hands has led to permanent loss of lands through sales to non-Maasai and commercial ventures. Geographer David Campbell has argued that it is the growing competition between farmers, herders, and wildlife in Kenya's Maasailand, and not pastoral practices themselves, which led to the increase of land degradation and problems of overgrazing. Both livestock and crops in Kajiado District were lost in the 1972–1973 drought, leading herders and farmers to seek new production techniques. Many younger educated Maasai have begun to grow crops and sell livestock, but the availability of fertile land limits this option to all but a few.[11]

The future for the Maasai will very likely see large changes in both their economic system of land use and social relations of production. Many of these changes have already begun. The Maasai have increasingly integrated into the cash market. Their diet includes substantial amounts of grain, sugar, tea, and cloth, all paid for by cash sales of both cattle and small stock. Some local Maasai groups, particularly those around the Amboseli game park, receive a portion of the park fees and hotel profits, which have been as high as $200,000 annually. And increasingly the Maasai have sent their children to public schools, where school leavers have entered wage employment in tourism, police and military, livestock marketing, and professional jobs through secondary and post secondary education.

However, the problem with increased commercial activity in Maasailand is that it will very likely lead to increased polarization between rich and poor Maasai, with a wealthy few able to purchase land titles and cattle, and many poor and landless Maasai end up as herding laborers or migrants to urban areas.

The question of impoverishment and polarization among subsistence pastoralists entering the market economy is a recurring theme in Kenya and is repeated in other case examples.

Turkana

In contrast to the Maasai who were strongly affected by commercial development, the Turkana remain the most isolated and mobile of all Kenya's pastoralists. However, they also have been the targets of one of the largest famine-relief efforts in Africa, and in the 1980s almost one third of the Turkana population were settled around famine-relief camps.

The Turkana number over 248,000 people (203,000 in Turkana District) and inhabit a grazing environment of 67,000 km², consisting mainly of scrub bushland and semi-desert in northwestern Kenya. Turkana District is a low-lying plain in the Great Rift Valley between 660 and 900 m above sea level and with very low ecological potential due to erratic and low rainfall. Lying on Kenya's northwest border with Uganda and Sudan, Turkana District is the most isolated and least developed in Kenya.[12]

The Turkana are highly nomadic, living in small household units (*awi*) consisting primarily of a male stockowner and his polygynous family. Each autonomous household is affiliated into one of nineteen territorial sections, providing safe and extensive environments for grazing and watering livestock. Like the Ariaal, Turkana live off the milk and meat of four types of stock—camels, cattle, goats, sheep—and keep donkeys for transportation of water and houses. There is some trade of livestock for grains, tea, and tobacco at small shops in the towns, but the lack of adequate roads and vast size of Turkana District have limited commercial activity among the Turkana. In addition to pastoralism, Turkana also engage in fishing and hunting-gathering, particularly during periods of drought; more recently they have responded to irrigated agricultural schemes and opportunities for wage-labor.[13]

The essential pastoral strategy of the Turkana stockowner is to subdivide his herds and his family and move them to places where resources are temporarily available. During the brief rainy seasons, neighborhoods of households and herds congregate in the lowland plains. These households separate during the dry season with the women and children of the *awi* remaining with the milk camels and small stock in the plains while the non-milk animals are dispersed into mobile satellite camps of age and species specific stock managed by adolescents and adult males. The long term study of the Ngisonyoka Turkana by the South Turkana Ecosystem Project[14] shows the high degree of Turkana nomadism: the *awi* moves from 5–10 times a year in distances ranging from 1–20 km (and occasionally up to 50km) in search of grazing and water for their livestock.

The Turkana have a reputation as fierce warriors who pushed their way into northwestern Kenya from Sudan in the 17th and 18th centuries to escape land pressures from the north, and took grazing lands from the Samburu, Rendille, and Dasenech during the past two centuries.[15] But the Turkana were virtually isolated from the world economy until the late 19th century when both Swahili and Arab traders traded firearms and tobacco for ivory, and armed forces under Menelik II attempted to incorporate the Turkana area into Ethiopia.

The British moved into the Turkana area primarily to stop Ethiopian military advances, incorporating Turkana into their colonial administration in 1902. From military posts at Lodwar and Lake Baringo the British periodically conducted punitive raids against the Turkana for cattle raiding. But outside attempts to control the Turkana through police actions and taxation, the British administration did little to encourage development or integrate the District into the larger colony. Until World War II, trade in Turkana was controlled by outsiders (usually Somali shopkeepers) and the only employment opportunities for Turkana were as government headmen or police recruits.[16]

This policy of government neglect in Turkana continued after Independence. Since the 1960's the major impact on Turkana life has not been the development of a commercial economy, as among the Maasai, but the effects of drought and the influx of famine-relief agencies. The drought of 1961 attracted some 11,000 Turkana to famine camps seeking relief grains. Twenty years later, following the drought of 1980, some 80,000 Turkana, nearly one half of the district's population of 169,400, sought famine-relief as over 90% of their cattle, 40% of the camels, and 80% of their small stock died.[17]

Famine in Turkana occurred in 1979–1980 when drought and corruption led to poor grain distribution in Turkana, causing 3000 herders to seek relief at the Catholic mission of Kakuma. Due to appeals by the Bishop of Lodwar to the large international development and news media community in Nairobi, television coverage of the Turkana's plight was broadcast internationally. The coverage was so effective that several American tele-evangelists continue to use the same footage shot in 1981 in their appeals for donations into the 1990s! In 1980, the government of Kenya and members of the European Economic Community (EEC), particularly the Netherlands, Norway, and West Germany, established the multi-million dollar Turkana Rehabilitation Project (TRP). By 1982 TRP was providing 180,000 kg of famine grains per week to 80,000 Turkana, creating eight large famine camps attracting pastoralists who quickly overgrazed the limited pasture. The 1984–1985 famine which ravaged northeastern Africa went largely unnoticed in Turkana due to the long-standing famine-relief efforts in the district.[18]

Seeking to reduce food dependency, TRP initiated several alternative subsistence schemes including small-scale irrigation schemes to settle destitute pastoralists, and Norway's disastrous attempt to build a fish processing plant on Lake Turkana. A Food for Work (FFW) program that contributed paid labor to ongoing irrigation, rural road, and tree-planting projects in the District was initiated. By 1985, only 15,000 Turkana were receiving famine relief, although one third of the district's pastoralists remained in or near the famine camps.

These newly urbanized residents engaged in a variety of means to obtain cash and food, including low-paying wage labor as watchmen, herders, house builders, or road crews, or engaged in small scale business including grocery stores, small hotels, or livestock trade. These ventures require capital, however, and success comes only to a few. For others, charcoal burning, brewing illegal beer, selling *miraa* (*catha edulis*, a stimulant plant grown on Mt. Kenya), or engaging in prostitution remain the only opportunity of earning money in the district. Increasingly many young men have migrated to larger towns of the south to seek jobs as night watchmen, an occupation Ian Hogg points out is becoming increasingly synonymous with northern pastoralists.[19]

C. Terrence McCabe summarizes the effects for the Turkana of settling around the camps:

"There is little hope for families who have settled in the famine camps to return to their former life. . . . The longer a herdowner remains in a famine camp the weaker his bonds become with the pastoralist community. His "safety net" becomes the government and the international donor agencies rather than his fellow pastoralists."[20]

Clearly the impact of millions of dollars of international assistance (estimated at US $2.5 million between 1986–1989) has not enabled the Turkana to support themselves, either by fishing, farming, or livestock production.[21] Their case, perhaps more than any other, illustrates the wastefulness and inappropriateness of existing development aid to pastoralists in Africa.

Rendille

The Rendille formerly grazed large herds of camels and small stock in the Kaisut and Chalbi Deserts of Marsabit District. As described earlier, Rendille are descended from Somali-speaking groups (although unlike Somalis they are non-Muslims) and resemble in both appearance and social organization their allies, the Samburu. As among the Maasai groups, the Rendille have a strong reputation for organized warfare, although their history is marked more by defensive fighting than predatory expansion.

The history of the Rendille in the twentieth century has been one of ever increasing restriction in movement, forced upon them both by the colonial and Kenyan governments, as well as threats to their security by raiding Turkana and Boran groups. Between 1920 and 1980, the total Rendille population increased from about 8000 to 13,000; during the same period their home range was reduced from 57,600 km² to 8000 km².[22] The current Rendille herding range is primarily around the former wet-season grazing resources of the Kaisut Desert around Korr and Kargi water holes, which were formerly only used a few months a year during the rainy seasons when annual grasses bloomed. Now the Rendille live here year round, and have overgrazed the scarce vegetation, forcing them to herd their animals in distant camps, while the adult and child population are highly dependent on store-bought grains or famine relief distributed by church missions.

Prior to the British imposition of "tribal" boundaries in the NFD after 1911, the various pastoralist groups of Marsabit District lived in dynamic rather than static communities, with relatively fluid societal boundaries of immigration and intermarriage. Following the disasters of the late 19th century, Rendille found themselves increasingly restricted in herding range by both Turkana expansions from the northwest and Boran and Gabra movements from the North. The British consolidated this restriction by confining the Rendille to certain fixed water holes in the southern region of the district, and by formal-izing their area through the Tribal Grazing Areas Act in 1919 which gave water points in the Chalbi Desert to the Gabra, Mt. Marsabit to the Boran, the eastern side of Lake Turkana to the Turkana and Dasenech. Rendille annual migrations were reduced from 131–294 km in 1923 to a range of 13–73 km in 1978.[23]

As the Rendille continued to lose their grazing resources, they increasingly settled around permanent water holes, which were developing in the 1930's and 40's as small trading towns and police posts including Laisamis and Archer's Post. After 1963, these centers attracted western missionaries, partic-ularly the Catholic Church (Marsabit Diocese) which, as described earlier, established churches and primary schools among the Rendille at Illaut, Lais-amis, and Marsabit, among the Gabra at North Horr and Maikona, and among the Dasenech at Ileret. The smaller African Inland Church (AIC) established stations at Logologo (below Marsabit town), Gatab on Mt. Kulal, and at Ngurunit in the Ndoto Mountains among the Ariaal and Dorrobo on the Samburu/Marsabit District border.

The local infrastructure created by these organizations enabled the district to responded quickly to the drought of 1968–1971. The Catholic Church of Marsabit Diocese in particular played a strong role as the Catholic Relief Services (CRS) were responsible for distributing all famine-relief (corn, rice, soy and dry milk) donated by the USAID and UNICEF. With renewed drought in 1973, the Marsabit Diocese established distribution facilities among the Rendille at the Kaisut water holes at Korr and Kargi, which by 1976 developed into permanent mission stations. However none had sufficient pasture to keep animals, and the poorer Rendille families who settled around the mission soon became permanent dependents, without animals and with little wage work. By 1986, well after the drought had ended, forty percent of the Rendille population was settled permanently around the mission towns of Korr, Kargi, and Laisamis.

Catholic missions at Korr, Kargi, and Laisamis have developed into small towns, with permanent water, medical facilities, and shops for trade. Yet none had sufficient pasture to keep animals, and the poorer Rendille families who settled around the mission soon became permanent dependents, without animals and with little wage work. In 1980, a permanent church, school, and clinic had been built at Korr, which was fast becoming a new town. Between 6000 and 12,000 Rendille congregated around Korr during the drought of 1982–1984. By 1986, well after the drought had ended, forty percent of the Rendille population were settled permanently around the mission towns of Korr, Kargi, and Laisamis.

Although some Rendille, particularly wealthy households with large camel herds, are able to subsist off their animals in settlements away from the missions, the majority of Rendille have entered semi-urban life with all its advantages and disadvantages. At one extreme this is represented by the prostitution and beer brewing at Laisamis' Sabamba Village (poor people's housing built by the Catholic Mission). Advantages include access to education and jobs, with many Rendille youth entering school in the past fifteen years. There is a growing number of secondary school leavers seeking entrance into university (there are currently about 15 Rendille at university) or employment with government services. Several recently educated Rendille have engaged in electoral politics, winning seats in both local county council elections and the larger national parliament.

Paid labor is difficult to find in Marsabit, and many town dwellers must seek incomes from trade (in livestock, shop-keeping, selling *mira'a*, or beer-brewing), or else find wage-work in other parts of the country. As with other Kenyan pastoralists, many Rendille youth with primary school education join the police, army, or Game Department; those without formal education migrate to the cities to seek work as watchmen and security guards (in Nairobi alone there is a community of over 100 Rendille men working or seeking work as night watchmen.)

Some Rendille have engaged in alternative forms of production, particularly in irrigated agriculture. In 1973 the AIC mission in conjunction with the National Christian Council of Kenya (NCCK) established an agricultural settlement at Songa on Marsabit Mountain to grow maize in small family plots irrigated from taps fed from a central pump off the Gof Bongole reservoir. Although their first years were difficult with poor harvests, by 1986 Songa was a stable community of close to 1000 people, with each household allotted 10 acres for maize production. (The project is now administered by the Ministry of Agriculture through funds from the EEC). Songa households supplement their income by keeping a few cattle and small stock, grazed in reserves used by the Ariaal settlement at Karare a few kilometers below, from which milk, hides, and meat are sold at Marsabit town. Despite Songa's success, there are not enough resources on Marsabit mountain to offer a new economy of irrigated farming for the larger Rendille, Ariaal, and Boran populations living in the area.

Today Rendille are in transition from a past as livestock herders to an unknown future as town dwellers and agropastoralists. The constriction of their herding environment has made continued subsistence off their animals a tenuous undertaking. It is sadly ironic that of all types of pastoral systems in Kenya, the Rendille's dependence on the camel, an animal that thrives in drought and desert conditions, is among the most threatened.

Summary

Historically, northern Kenyan pastoralists survived in arid lands via pastoral livestock production by a variety of strategies including herd and household mobility characterized by individual stock ownership and communal land use; diversifying herd types and separating herds into different areas; and the formation and maintenance of social ties through descent, marriage, and stock alliances.

These safety mechanisms have broken down in the past fifty years due to a variety of factors. The Maasai lost pastoral lands to colonial appropriation (who confiscated a third of Maasai grazing lands to develop commercial ranches), to encroachment by agricultural groups expanding into semi-arid areas, and to the creation of tourist game parks. The Turkana have not lost grazing lands as the Maasai, but many were encouraged to give up nomadic pastoralism and settle around missions distributing famine-relief foods, a practice that continued long after drought crises had passed. The Rendille also settled around mission centers, driven not so much by drought as by severe restriction of their herding range by colonial grazing restrictions, inter-pastoralist warfare, and civil unrest during the *shifta* war.

The Ariaal have not faced large-scale herding restrictions, the instability of civil war, nor the expansion of agriculturalists or commercial growers in their area. They have been able to continue their pastoral economy, and may have some breathing space for some time. Ariaal pastoralism represents a viable food production system in Africa's arid regions, and if it is not disrupted, their animals can continue to provide their population with food and surplus for trade. The future lies in to what degree Ariaal pastoralism is aided, or conversely to what degree it is disrupted, by the development efforts of the missions and international donor agencies.

Notes

1. Spear [In press].
2. Waller 1988.
3. Holland 1987; Jacobs 1980a, 1980b.
4. Campbell 1986.
5. Holland 1987.
6. Galaty 1981b:81.
7. Group ranches discussed in Bennett 1984, 1988; Campbell 1984, 1986; Galaty 1980, 1981c; Halderman 1972; Hedlund 1971, 1979.
8. Oxby 1981:44–56.
9. Jacobs 1980a:292.
10. Galaty 1981b:82.
11. Campbell 1984, 1986.
12. Republic of Kenya 1984b.
13. Descriptions of the Turkana are found in Gulliver 1955, 1975; McCabe 1983, 1985, 1987a, 1987b.
14. Dyson-Hudson and McCabe 1985; McCabe et al.1988.
15. Lamphear 1976, 1988; Sobania 1980a.
16. Hogg 1986:319.
17. Hogg 1982.
18. McCabe 1988.
19. Hogg 1986.
20. McCabe 1988:17.
21. Adams 1986:323.
22. Sobania 1980b.
23. Sobania 1988:238.

Conclusion: Things Don't Necessarily Fall Apart

8 Over the past one hundred years, Ariaal have survived in Kenya's arid north by a generalist pastoral strategy raising camels, cattle, goats and sheep for subsistence and trade. Ariaal forged their identity during the hardships of the late nineteenth century when immigrant families from Rendille, Samburu, Maasai, and Boran banded together to recover from drought, famine and war.

Ariaal continue to survive by adapting to modern conditions of environmental stress and social dislocations. The past twenty years have seen dislocations of a new type with the rise of mission towns, increased political insecurity, and extensive integration into a burgeoning capitalist economy in Marsabit District. While these changes have presented new hazards including impoverishment and dependency on famine-relief, they have also offered new opportunities in wage labor and livestock marketing as well as improvements in the quality of life resulting from increased health care and educational opportunities. Ariaal have not "fallen apart", to borrow Chinua Achebe's phrase,[1] but have continued their pastoral system, pursuing their generalist strategy as they adapt to the new conditions of towns, increased marketing, and new employment opportunities.

There are a few important conclusions to draw from the Ariaal example which relate to how other African populations can endure in the perilous period ahead of global warming, population growth, and insurmountable debt in the global economy. These populations' ability to survive depends ultimately on much larger events in the world, particularly whether the western industrial countries continue to maintain unequal trading relations with the less developed world, and whether they continue to pollute the atmosphere and contribute to global warming at the current suicidal pace.

The first conclusion to draw is that there are few alternative food production systems possible in the arid regions of northern Africa outside that of livestock pastoralism. Pastoral production is a complex and finely tuned adaptation to arid lands and is perhaps the only way a majority of people can survive in an environment of less than 500 mm of rain annually. As rainfall is patchy and erratic, the pastoralists must be able to move their animals over a wide distance to take advantage of seasonal and short lived grazing resources, allowing them to convert variable resources into a steady supply of food in terms of milk, meat, and livestock to trade for grains, tea and sugar that does not grow in the region.

Agriculture is a possibility in certain parts of Marsabit District, and the development of irrigated maize fields and gardens on Marsabit Mountain and at Ngurunit represents important alternative food strategies that need to be developed. But it is very unlikely that the finite water resources of these highland areas can support the district's growing population through agriculture, at least not with the existing technology. Perhaps future improvements in solar and wind power, water conservation, superconductors, and the development of new crop varieties will aid food production in Africa's arid lands, but these developments are at least twenty to fifty years away. In the meantime, livestock pastoralism remains the most productive way to feed the majority of Marsabit's rural population.

Unfortunately, both the missions and UNESCO-IPAL project refused to recognize this fundamental fact in the implementation of their development plans. I once asked a priest at the Catholic Mission at Korr what will these settled Rendille eat now that they cannot keep their animals, and he replied, "Let them grow vegetable gardens like we do!" But the church's vegetable garden is fed directly from the mission well, and there is not enough water in Korr to support gardens for all the town's residents.

The majority of people living in the mission towns of Korr and Laisamis are quite poor, many having been driven to settle there by loss of livestock in the droughts of the 1970s and 1980s. Those town households who have animals must herd them in distant areas and depend on their sale to purchase foods to feed their town members. Many residents of the towns, such as the blacksmith families at Korr or Dorrobo gatherers at Ngurunit, have never owned more than a few animals; others are more recently impoverished by the droughts. Still others are pursuing lifestyles independent of pastoralism, such as educated Rendille or Somalis keeping shops, engaged in trading, or working for the government or missions as clerks, teachers, or manual workers.

Nevertheless the economic basis of the community—livestock production—is seriously undermined in these urban areas. There are several exceptions to this pattern. Town dwellers at Ngurunit and on Marsabit Mountain at Karare village do keep large herds of animals, and their standard of living and nutritional status is better for it. But it is questionable how long the resources can support these herds if these towns continue to grow.

IPAL's solution to the food problem was a bit different than that of the missions: "Let them sell their annual surplus of animals and purchase grains." This position falls more in line with development interests of Kenya as well as policies of the international donor community which promotes agricultural marketing to provide food security through crisis periods.[2] But here, too, IPAL did not appreciate the fact that poor people sell a much larger proportion of their animals than do the wealthy to buy food, and that the poorest people with few or no animals are forced to live in towns outside the pastoral economy.

IPAL and its successors in the Ministry of Livestock Development are fundamentally concerned with increasing commercial rather than subsistence production, and their policies are aimed mainly at benefiting the private entrepreneur who buys tle and goats, holds them for fattening, then sells at a profit to butchers or ranches in the south.

The creation of livestock marketing centers has benefited local entrepreneurs and members of county councils who control trade, butcheries, and marketing at the expense of the poorer pastoralist producers. Although not as pronounced as among the Boran of Isiolo town, new classes of urban entrepreneurs and poorer wage-workers and hired herders are emerging among Rendille and Ariaal in Marsabit District. The polarization of pastoralists into "haves" and "have-nots" is a trend reported for many societies in Africa including Fulani, Tuareg, Somalis, Boran, Maasai and Samburu.[3] Although Marsabit District has not undergone privatization of the range and the spread of individual ranches as among Maasai and Samburu, there are signs that commercial livestock production is concentrating in fewer hands, driving many poor pastoralists out of the economy and into towns to seek wage labor, usually at the lowest rungs of the economic ladder.

Development Approaches to Pastoralism

Assistance projects undertaken by both international development agencies and private voluntary organizations have followed three distinct approaches in Africa's pastoral regions: 1) the promotion of commercial production coupled with restrictions of traditional pastoral practices; 2) the provision of massive food aid and famine relief; and (least often) 3) supports for the traditional pastoral economy with improvements in animal husbandry, veterinary care, and range conservation.

The replacement of traditional livestock practices by western commercial systems is the most prevalent form of development assistance, and is widely promoted by international development agencies including the World Bank, USAID, and the European Economic Community (EEC). These donor agencies focus aid to projects that develop the market infrastructure, including construction of offices and providing salaries to government employees, building roads and abbatoirs, introducing technological improvements in veterinary care, milking and beef production, and creating private or parastatal ranches to fence in the range and restrict non-ranch livestock. Internationally assisted ranches have been developed in Botswana, Zambia, Niger, Nigeria, Tanzania and Kenya, with the emphasis on export production, exemplified by Botswana selling most of its beef to the EEC. In Kenya, ranches were developed in Maasailand in the 1960s and in Samburu District in the 1970's to produce beef for the growing urban markets.

In northern Kenya international aid donors have concentrated on improvement of the marketing infrastructure through the establishment of mechanized wells, local auctions, improvements in transportation, and the imposition of grazing restrictions to protect the range. This approach has been the main policy of the German-funded IPAL project in Marsabit District.

Ariaal elders discuss livestock at Lewogoso

The major problem with the international donor approach is that it starts from the needs of the donor country and not from that of the recipients of the aid. The World Bank and USAID represent western capitalist interests and are mainly concerned with increasing export revenues from less developed countries to pay off debts and enable the donor country to export expensive foreign technology and personnel. They favor policies promoting agricultural and mineral exports from the rural areas to the cities and from the less developed countries to the developed world.

Michael Horowitz, a former consultant with USAID and director of the Institute for Developmental Anthropology, has argued that the principal reason expensive development projects fail in pastoral areas of Africa is that invariably planning is from the top down, usually formulated in European or American capitals with few consultations with local people as to their specific needs. These development projects tend to favor high cost technological improvements such as roads or well mechanization, but seldom appreciate the impact these improvements have at the local level.[4]

This is certainly true of the UNESCO-IPAL project. For example, IPAL recommended grazing restrictions and mechanization of local wells without considering the consequences of limiting pastoral mobility, the pastoralists' main strategy of coping with drought conditions. Grazing restrictions, the creation of bounded ranches, or the concentration of populations around mechanized water holes lead in fact to further overgrazing and environmental degradation, the situation IPAL was designed to prevent.

International development agencies implicitly assumed a stereotyped portrait of the pastoralist as "irrational", wanting only to increase his herds at all costs, and wasteful, freely overgrazing unless restrictions were imposed. It is a wonder, Horowitz writes, how a people practicing so "self-destructive" an economy could have survived for so long or at all![5] Climatic evidence shows that there has been a steady decline in rainfall since the late 1960s throughout Africa caused by forces much larger than pastoral overgrazing or overpopulation in the arid regions.

A second approach in international aid concentrates on the provision of famine relief, principally as donated food grains, to pastoralists during drought conditions. Famine-relief has been the main approach of the Catholic Church in Marsabit District, and it's periodic distribution since 1973 has led to sedentarized Rendille populations at Korr, Kargi, and Laisamis.

Oxfam International, a major relief organization, has been strongly critical of long term famine-relief projects.[6] These projects concentrate on the wholesale distribution of relief foods, which may last long after the crisis has passed, and lead to the formation of permanent and dependent populations. Donated grains intended as food supplements quickly become the primary food source for settled populations, replacing local food production and ultimately leading to greater malnutrition. Massive famine-relief efforts are an inappropriate and destructive form of development assistance. Like other progressive relief organizations, Oxfam concentrates on assisting people to feed themselves by providing low-cost technical assistance, improving traditional food production techniques, and searching for alternatives to traditional foods.

Much of Oxfam's criticisms apply to the Catholic Relief Services and their work in Marsabit District. The towns of Korr and Kargi developed from famine-relief distribution points sponsored by the Catholic Churches at Laisamis and Marsabit in the early 1970s. By 1980 they were home to permanently settled Rendille constituting 45% of the total Rendille population. Among these settled Rendille, traditional foods of milk and meat have been largely replaced by less nutritious grains. The Marsabit Diocese is self-critical of their creation of dependent Rendille populations around their missions at Korr, Kargi, and Laisamis, and they have reassessed their initial aid programs, providing food aid only during food crises and only to the most destitute people. Nevertheless, the efforts of the Catholic Church in education, health care, and religious services continue to be aimed at the settled pastoralist communities. They have not developed, nor are they likely to develop, Rendille livestock and grazing.

A final approach in livestock development and the one least taken is to offer direct assistance to subsistence pastoralists by providing veterinary care for domestic animals and health care for their human herders, improving stock through selective breeding, and training pastoralists in livestock management and veterinary skills. An example of this approach was IPAL's Traditional Livestock Management Project which introduced low-cost veterinary medicines and training in their administration. The proposed camel extension project of GTZ (German Development Corporation) intends to carry on this work among Rendille and Ariaal in Korr.

Examples of direct aid to pastoralists include the camel restocking programs in Korr and North Horr, funded by private religious organizations including Food for the Hungry and World Vision. The AIC in Ngurunit and Marsabit have also focused their work on providing technical assistance to local pastoralists in both water development and, more recently, veterinary care and training in camel production.

The purpose of these missionary efforts are unashamedly religious. Nevertheless, private voluntary organizations such as the AIC and the nonreligious Oxfam have provided the most direct assistance to the pastoralists in terms of improving the traditional livestock production system.

The Future

The future of pastoral peoples is not good. Trends throughout Africa point to an increasing inability of pastoralists to feed themselves in arid lands.

Pastoralists are pressured from several directions. Increased population growth, particularly of neighboring agriculturalists expanding into pastoral areas but also of pastoral populations themselves, threatens the pastoralists' ability to live off their herds. This population pressure does not occur in the form predicted by neo-Malthusians (i.e., of overpopulation leading to mass starvation) but by pastoralists facing increasing restrictions on their herding range by commercial expansion, the development of tourist game parks, and the appropriation of the best land by private ranchers. Population growth is a problem affecting all populations in Africa including pastoralists, and access to family planning services is a growing concern in African development. Unfortunately those seeking birth control devices in Marsabit District health clinics may be offered little more than a calendar.

A second problem threatening pastoralists is the spread of AIDS in Africa. Although there is little research on the incidence of AIDS in pastoralist regions, the epidemic is spreading from urban concentrations to rural areas with devastating speed. Given the poor medical resources in Marsabit District, and AIDS heterosexual transmission (aggravated by high rates of venereal disease), it is certain that AIDS will take a toll among Rendille and Ariaal as well as other rural Kenyan populations.

A third danger is the dramatic increase in global warming in the past twenty years and the threat of renewed drought and famine in Africa. The greenhouse effect is brought about largely by the burning of fossil fuels and the release of chloro-fluoro-carbons in the atmosphere. While some of the greenhouse effect is a result of deforestation and fuel burning in the less developed countries, the overwhelming majority of greenhouse gases emanate from the industrialized countries of the developed north, both western and eastern hemisphere. Climatic changes that led to famine in Africa in the 1970s and 1980s are certain to increase as the world warms and air and ocean currents shift. Pastoralists of northern Kenya have little control over these changes, but those of us in a position to influence industrial policy can do something to conserve the world's dwindling resources.

The problems of population growth, AIDS, and global warming are enormous. However there are signs that these catastrophes can be avoided as efforts by governments, agencies, and individuals increase to provide family planning services, conserve fossil fuels, and engage in medical research and health care delivery to the world's poorer regions.

A Few Proposals

If the world can hang on, pastoralists such as the Ariaal do have a chance to survive and exist in the arid regions. However, their ability to survive drought and development will improve if a few policies are followed.

Development planners and government agencies need to appreciate that pastoral production systems are the result of generations of adaptive behavior and knowledge by populations in arid lands. Developers must observe how the traditional livestock economy is practiced, and formulate policies for technical and economic assistance through consultation with the pastoralists themselves. After all, it is the camel, cattle, and small stock pastoralists themselves who are the true experts of food production in arid regions.

Development agencies need to concentrate their efforts in pastoral regions on animal production, just as agricultural assistance focuses on the needs of the farmer. Veterinary services must be expanded to provide low-cost medicines and training in their administration; government needs to learn from successful examples of pest and parasite control such as eradication of tsetse in other parts of Africa. Mobile veterinary and human health clinics need to contact pastoral settlements on a regular basis to provide low-cost antibiotics, vaccinations, and preventative health care to both human and animal populations.

Grazing restrictions should not be imposed in and of themselves as a solution, as they are impossible to achieve and result in further decline of pastoral herd viability. The solution to overgrazing is to enable pastoral herds to disperse over wide areas and away from urban centers. This can be achieved by a rational policy of water development and the provision of public security guaranteeing safety from theft. Mobility of the herding and livestock populations should be encouraged rather than discouraged.

Market infrastructure should be improved by making stock routes, auctions, and competitive marketing available to the pastoralist. Cooperatives for transporting and selling livestock should be encouraged, with profits used to hire drivers, veterinary officers, and security. Extension services in education, business and accounting skills, and livestock management should be increased.

Given developments in urban migration, sedentarization, and population growth, it is unlikely that the pastoral economy can sustain all its people. New job opportunities related to the economic growth of the district should be encouraged, and appropriate training offered. It is particularly important to train local health, veterinary, and marketing officers recruited directly from the pastoralists themselves.

Institutions empowering the rural pastoralists need to be strengthened, both in political and economic arenas. This includes democratically elected representatives from the local settlement, town councils, county council, and parliamentary seats, a policy that is presently in effect in Kenya. But more than political office, pastoralists need to control their own resources. In particular herding cooperatives with marketing quotas and fair prices set, and banking institutions rewarding savings and offering low-cost credits, would enable the pastoralists to have some security against the vagaries of environmental stress and economic hardship.

Finally, efforts to promote conservation need to be supported and expanded. Tree planting is a positive example of a conservation effort that is having a visible effect in the new towns of Korr and Ngurunit. Implemented mainly by private agencies including the Children's Christian Fund and InterAid, barren desert towns such as Korr are being transformed as hardy acacia trees line the streets and people's yards, offering shade, protection against wind, and most importantly firewood, the region's only fuel.

I asked my friend Lugi Lengesen what he thought of the changes that have affected Ariaal life including the missions, the schools, and the UNESCO project. He replied,

"This is not good land to grow corn or raise gardens. That is something people in the south know how to do very well. But we Ariaal know how to grow our cattle and camels, we know this land because it is our farm. Give us veterinary medicines for our animals, medicine for our infants, schools to educate our children in livestock and health, and markets and transportation to sell our animals. Then places like Korr can become beautiful."

Notes

1. Chinua Achebe's classic novel *Things Fall Apart* (1958) describes the irreversible impact of colonialism on Ibo (Nigeria) culture.

2. See for example World Bank 1981, 1984, 1986, 1990.

3. See for example Campbell 1984; Dahl and Hjort 1979; Galaty 1981a; Hogg 1986; Hjort 1981; Little 1985; Sperling 1987a; Swift 1977.

4. Horowitz 1979:88–89.

5. Horowitz 1979:24.

6. Jackson and Eade 1982:11.

Bibliography

Achebe, Chinua. 1958. *Things Fall Apart*. Oxford: Heinemann.

Adams, M. 1986. Merging Relief and Development: The case of the Turkana. *Development Policy Review*. 4:314-24.

Ambrose, S.H. 1982. Archeology and Linguistic Reconstructions of History in East Africa. IN C. Ehret and M. Posnansky (eds.) *The Archeological and Linguistic Reconstruction of African History*. Pp.104-157. Berkeley: University of California Press.

Barth, F. 1956. Ecologic Relationships of Ethnic Groups in Swat, North Pakistan. *American Anthropologist* 58:1079-1089.

Beaman, A.W. 1981. *The Rendille Age-set System in Ethnographic Context*. Ph.D. Dissertation, Boston University.

Bennett, J.W. 1984. *Political Ecology and Development Projects affecting Pastoralist Peoples in East Africa*. Madison: Land Tenure Center, University of Wisconsin.

Bennett, J. W. 1988. The Political Ecology and Economic Development of Migratory Pastoralist Societies in Eastern Africa. IN D. W. Attwood, T. C. Bruneau, and J. G. Galaty (eds.) *Power and Poverty*, pp. 51-60. Boulder: Westview Press.

Berntsen, J.L. 1976. The Maasai and Their Neighbors: Variables of Interaction. *African Economic History* 2:1-11.

Berntsen. J.L. 1979. *Pastoralism, Raiding, and Prophets: Masailand in the 19th Century*. Ph.D. Dissertation. University of Wisconsin.

Bourgeot, A. 1981. Nomadic Pastoral Society and the Market: The Penetration of the Sahel by Commercial Relations. IN J.G. Galaty and P.C. Salzman (eds.) *Change and Development in Nomadic and Pastoral Societies*. Pp. 116-127. Leiden: E.J. Brill.

Bradburd, D. 1980. Never Give a Shepherd an Even Break: Class and Labor among the Komachi. *American Ethnologist* 7(4): 603-620.

Brown, L. R. and E. C. Wolf 1985. *Reversing Africa's Decline*. Worldwatch paper 65. Washington, D.C.: Worldwatch Institute.

Campbell, D. J. 1984. Responses to Drought Among Farmers and Herders in Southern Kajiado District, Kenya. *Human Ecology* 12(1):35-64.

Campbell, D. J. 1986. The Prospect for Desertification in Kajiado District, Kenya. *Geography Journal* 152(1):44-55.

Carles, A.B. 1980. Productivity Levels of the Goat Herd at Ngurunit. *IPAL Technical Report A-3*. Pp.62-73. Nairobi: UNESCO-MAB Integrated Project in Arid Lands.

Chanler, W.A. 1896. *Through Jungle and Desert, Travels in Eastern Africa*. London: MacMillan Publ. Ltd.

Cossins, N.J. 1985. The Productivity and Potential of Pastoral Systems. *ILCA Bulletin* 21:10-15. Nairobi: International Livestock Centre for Africa.

Dahl, G. 1979a. Ecology and Equality: the Boran Case. In Equipe Ecologie et Anthropologie des Societes Pastorales (ed.) *Pastoral Production and Society*, pp. 261-281. Cambridge: Cambridge University Press.

Dahl, G. 1979b. *Suffering Grass: Subsistence and Society of Waso Borana*. Stockholm Studies in Social Anthropology 8. Stockholm: University of Stockholm.

Dahl, G. and A. Hjort. 1976. *Having Herds: Pastoral Herd Growth and Household Economy*. Stockholm Studies in Social Anthropology 2. Stockholm: Dept. of Social Anthropology, University of Stockholm.

Dahl, G. and A. Hjort. 1979. *Pastoral Change and the Role of Drought*. SAREC Report R2:1979. Stockholm: Swedish Agency for Research Cooperation with Developing Countries.

Dyson-Hudson, N. 1972. The Study of Nomads. *Journal of Asian and African Studies* 7:2-29.

Dyson-Hudson, N. and R. Dyson-Hudson. 1982. The Structure of East African Herds and the Future of East African Herders. *Development and Change*. Vol 13:213-238.

Dyson-Hudson, R. 1980. Toward a General Theory of Pastoralism and Social Stratification. *Nomadic Peoples* 7:1-7.

Dyson-Hudson, R. and J. T. McCabe. 1985. South Turkana Nomadism: Coping with an Unpredictably Varying Environment. *Human Relations Area Files Ethnography series FL 17-001*. New Haven: HRAF.

Ehret, C. 1971. *Southern Nilotic History: Linguistic Approaches to the Study of the Past*. Evanston: Northwestern University Press.

Ehret, C. 1974. *Ethiopians and East Africans: The Problem of Contacts*. Nairobi: East African Literature Bureau.

Ehret, C. 1984. Historical/Linguistic Evidence for Early African Food Production. IN J.D. Clark and S.A. Brandt (eds.) *From Hunters to Farmers*, Pp. 26-35. Berkeley: University of California Press.

Ehrlich, P. R., A. H. Ehrlich and J. P. Holdren. 1973. *Human Ecology: Problems and Solutions*. San Francisco: W. H. Freeman and Co.

Eicher, C. K. 1986. Strategic Issues in Combating Hunger and Poverty in Africa. IN R. J. Bert and J. S. Whitaker (eds.) *Strategies for African Development*, pp. 242-75. Berkeley: University of California Press.

Evans-Pritchard, E.E. 1940. *The Nuer* Oxford: Clarendon Press.

FAO 1950. *Production Yearbook*. Rome: Food and Agriculture Organization of the United Nations.

FAO 1990. *Production Yearbook*. Rome: Food and Agriculture Organization of the United Nations.

Field, C. R. 1979. Preliminary Report on Ecology and Management of Camels, Sheep and Goats in Northern Kenya. *IPAL Technical Report E-1a*, Nairobi: UNESCO.

Field, C.R. 1985. Introduction: Control and Productivity in the Arid Lands of Northern Kenya. *IPAL Technical Report E-7*. Nairobi: UNESCO.

Field, C.R. and S.P. Simpkin 1985. The Importance of Camels to Subsistence Pastoralists in Kenya. *IPAL Technical Report E-7* Pp. 161–192. Nairobi: UNESCO.

Fleming, H.C. 1965. *The Age-Grading Cultures of East Africa: An Historical Inquiry*. Ph.D. Dissertation, University of Pittsburgh.

Franke, R. W. and B. Chasin. 1980. *Seeds of Famine: Ecological Destruction and the Development Dilemma in the West African Sahel*. Montclair: Montclair Press.

Frantz, C. 1980. The Open Niche, Pastoralism, and Sedentarization in the Mambila grasslands of Nigeria. IN P. C. Salzman (ed.) *When Nomads Settle*, pp. 62-79. NY: J. F. Bergin Publishers.

Fratkin, E. 1986. Stability and Resilience in East African Pastoralism: The Ariaal and Rendille of Northern Kenya. *Human Ecology* 14(3):269-286.

Fratkin, E. 1987a. *The Organization of Labor and Production Among the Ariaal Rendille, Nomadic Pastoralists of Northern Kenya.* Ph.D. Dissertation, the Catholic University of America.

Fratkin, E. 1987b. Age-sets, Households and the Organization of Pastoral Production. *Research in Economic Anthropology* 8:295-314.

Fratkin, E. 1989a. Household Variation and Gender Inequality in Ariaal Rendille Pastoral Production: Results of a Stratified Time Allocation Survey. *American Anthropologist* 91(2):45-55.

Fratkin, E. 1989b. Two lives for the Ariaal. *Natural History*, 98(5):39-49.

Fratkin E. 1991. The Loibon as Sorcerer: A Samburu Loibon Among the Ariaal Rendille 1973-1987. *Africa* Vol. 60 No.3.

Fratkin, E. [In Press]. Maa- Speakers of the Northern Desert: Recent Developments in Ariaal and Rendillle Identity. IN T. Spear and R. Waller (eds.) *Being Maasai: Ethnicity and Identity in East Africa.* London: James Currey.

Fratkin, E. and E.A. Roth [In Press]. Drought and Economic Differentiation Among Ariaal Pastoralists of Kenya *(Human Ecology)*.

Galaty, J. G. 1980. The Maasai Group Ranch: Politics and Development in an African Pastoral Society. IN P. C. Salzman (ed.) *When Nomads Settle: Processes of Sedenterization as Adaptation and Response*, pp. 157-72. NY: J. F. Bergin Publishers, Inc.

Galaty, J. G. 1981a. Introduction: Nomadic Pastoralists and Social Change. IN J. G. Galaty and P. C. Salzman (eds.) *Change and Development in Nomadic and Pastoral Societies*, pp. 4-26. Leiden: C. J. Brill.

Galaty, J. G. 1981b. Land and Livestock among Kenyan Maasai. IN J. G. Galaty and P. C. Salzman (eds.) *Change and Development in Nomadic and Pastoralist Societies*, pp. 68-88. Leiden: E. J. Brill.

Galaty, J. G. 1981c. Organizations for Pastoral Development: Contexts of Causality, Change and Assessment. IN J. Galaty, D. Aronson and P. Salzman (eds.) *The Future of Pastoral Peoples.* Pp. 284-293. Ottawa: International Development Research Centre.

Galvin, K. 1985. *Food Procurement, Diet, Activities and Nutrition in an Ecological and Social Context.* Ph.D. Dissertation, Department of Anthropology, SUNY-Binghamton

Glantz, M. H. (ed.). 1987a. *Drought and Hunger in Africa: Denying Famine a Future.* Cambridge University Press.

Glantz, M. H. 1987b. Drought in Africa. *Scientific American* 256:34-40.

Goldschmidt, W. 1971. Independence as an Element in Pastoral Social Systems. *Anthropology Quarterly* 44:132-142.

Grandin, B. E. 1988. Wealth and Pastoral Dairy Production: A Case study from Maasailand. *Human Ecology* 16(1):1-21.

Gulliver, P.H. 1955. *The Family Herds.* London: Routledge and Kegan Paul Ltd.

Gulliver, P.H. 1975. Nomadic movement: Its Causes and Implications. IN T. Monod (ed.) *Pastoralism in Tropical Africa.* London: Oxford University Press.

Halderman, J.M. 1972. Analysis of Continued Nomadism on the Kaputiei Maasai Group Ranches: Social and Ecological Factors. *Institute for Development Studies Discussion paper 152.* Nairobi: University of Nairobi.

Hardin, G. 1968. The Tragedy of the Commons. *Science* 162:1243-48.

Hedlund, H. G. B. 1971. *The Impact of Group Ranches on Pastoral Society.* IDS Staff Paper No. 100, Institute of Development Studies. Nairobi: University of Nairobi.

Hedlund, H. G. B. 1979. Contradictions in the Peripherization of a Pastoral Society: The Maasai. *Review of African Political Economy* 15/16:15-34.

Heine, B. 1976. Notes on the Rendille Language (Kenya). *Afrika und Ubersee, Sprachen-Kulturen.* 59(3):176–223.

Heine, B. 1979. Some Linguistic Observations of the Early History of Africa. *Sprache und Geschichte in Afrika.* 1:37–54.

Heine, B., F. Rottland, and R. Vossen 1979. Proto-Baz: Some Aspects of Early Nilotic-Cushitic Contacts. *Sprache und Geshichte in Afrika* 1:75–91.

Hjort, A. 1979. *Savanna Town: Rural Ties and Urban Opportunities in Northern Kenya.* Stockholm Studies in Social Anthropology Vol. 7. Stockholm: University of Stockholm.

Hjort, A. 1981. A Critique of Ecological Models of Pastoral Land Use. *Ethnos* 46(3–4):171–189.

Hogg, R. 1982. Destitution and Development: The Turkana of Northwest Kenya. *Disasters* 6(3):164–168.

Hogg, R. 1986. The New Pastoralism: Poverty and Dependency in Northern Kenya. *Africa* 56(3):319–333.

Holland, K. 1987. *Land, Livestock, and People: New Demographic Considerations for Kajiado Maasai.* Discussion paper No. 5, East African Pastoral Systems Project, Department of Anthropology, McGill University.

Horowitz, M. M. 1979. *The Sociology of Pastoralism and African Livestock Projects.* AID Program Evaluation Discussion Paper No. 6, The Studies Division, Office of Evaluation, Bureau for Program and Policy Coordination. Washington: United States Agency for International Development.

Ingold, T. 1980. *Hunters, Pastoralists and Ranchers: Reindeer Economies and Their Transformations.* Cambridge: Cambridge University Press.

IPAL 1976. UNEP-MAB Integrated Project in Arid Lands (IPAL) Phase III. (1977-1980). *Regional Project Document* FR/1101-77. Nairobi: UNESCO-IPAL.

IPAL 1984. Integrated Resource Assessment and Management Plan for Western Marsabit District, Northern Kenya. *IPAL Technical Report No. A-6.* Nairobi: UNESCO.

IPAL 1985. *Camel Diseases and Productivity in the Arid Lands of Northern Kenya. IPAL Technical Report No. E-7.* Nairobi: Integrated Project in Arid Lands.

Jackson, T. and D. Eade. 1982. *Against the Grain.* London: Oxfam.

Jacobs, A. H. 1965. *The Traditional Political Organzation of the Pastoral Massai.* D.Phil. Dissertation, Oxford University.

Jacobs, A. H. 1965. African Pastoralists: Some General Remarks. *Anthropology Quarterly* 38:144–54.

Jacobs, A.H. 1980a. Pastoral Development in Tanzanian Maasailand. *Rural Africana* 7:1–15.

Jacobs, A.H. 1980b. Pastoral Maasai and Tropical Rural Development. In. R.Bates and M. Lofchie (eds.) *Agricultural Development in Africa: Issues in Public Policy.* NY: Praeger Publishers.

Kadenyi, E. 1983. *A Report on Incidence of Disease among the Nomadic and Sedentarized Rendille of Marsabit-Northern Kenya.* Nairobi: UNESCO Integrated Project in Arid Lands.

KALRES 1985. *Report of the Tripartite Review Mission on the Kenya Arid Lands Research Station (KALRES),* 3–11 February 1985. Nairobi: UNESCO-MAB.

Kelly, R. C. 1985. *The Nuer Conquest.* Ann Arbor: University of Michigan Press.

Lamphear, J. 1976. *The Traditional History of the Jie of Uganda.* Oxford: Clarendon Press.

Lamphear, J. 1988. The People of the Grey Bull: The Origin and Expansion of the Turkana. *Journal of African History* 29:27–33.

Lamprey, H.F. 1976. *The UNEP-MAB Integrated Project in Arid Lands: Phase III Kenya 1977–1980.* Regional Project Document FP/1101-77. Nairobi: United Nations Environment Programme

Lamprey, H. F. 1983. Pastoralism Yesterday and Today: The Overgrazing Problem. IN F. Bourliere (ed.) *Tropical Savannas,* pp. 643-666. Vol. 13 Ecosystems of the World. Amsterdam: Elsevier.

Lamprey, H. F. and H. Yusuf. 1981. Pastoralism and Desert Encroachment in N. Kenya. *Ambio* 10(2–3):131–34.

Little, P. D. 1985. Social differentiation and pastoralist sedentarization in N. Kenya. *Africa* 55(3):243–61.

Lonsdale, J.M. 1970. European attitudes and African Pressures: Missions and government in Kenya Between the Wars. IN B.A. Ogot (ed.) *Hadith 2.* pp. 229-242. Nairobi: East African Literature Bureau

Malthus, T.R. 1958 (1798). *Essay on the Principle of Population.* Lonson: Dent and Sons.

Markovitz, M.D. 1973. *The Cross and the Sword.* Standford: Hoover Institution Press.

McCabe, J. T. 1983. Land Use Among the Pastoral Turkana. *Rural Africana* 15–16:109–126.

McCabe, J.T. 1985. *Livestock management Among the Turkana: A Social and Ecological Analysis of Herding in an East African Pastoral Population.* Ph.D. Dissertation, State University of New York at Binghampton.

McCabe, J. T. 1987a. Inter-household Variation in Livestock Production in S. Turkana District, Kenya. *Research in Economic Anthropology* 8:277–93.

McCabe, J.T. 1987b. Drought and Recovery: Livestock Dynamics Among the Ngisonyoka Turkana of Kenya. *Human Ecology* 15(4):371–385.

McCabe, J. T. 1988. *Blessing or Curse: The Impact of Famine Relief on Traditional Means of Coping with Drought Among the Pastoral Turkana of Kenya.* Unpublished manuscript, Department of Anthropology, University of Georgia

McCabe, J.T., R. Dyson-Hudson, P.W. Leslie, N. Dyson-Hudson, J. Wienpahl 1988. Movement and Migration as Pastoral Responses to Limited and Unpredictable Resources. IN Whitehead, Hutchinson, Tinnmann and Varady (eds.) *Arid Lands Today and Tomorrow,* pp. 727–34. Boulder: Westview Press.

Nathan, M.A. and E. Fratkin 1990. *Health and Nutritional Consequences of Recent Sedentarization of Rendille Pastoralists in Northern Kenya.* Paper presented to 1990 African Studies Association meetings, Baltimore MD.

Nicholson, S. E. 1979. The Method of Historical Climate Reconstruction and its Application to Africa. *Journal of African History* 20:31–49.

Nicholson, S. E. 1980. The Nature of Rainfall Fluctuation in Subtropical West Africa. *Monthly Weather Review* 108:473–87.

Njiru, G.K. 1984. Marketing and Infrastructure, IN *IPAL Technical Report Number A-6,* Nairobi: UNESCO-FRG-MAB Integrated Project in Arid Lands.

O'Leary, M. F. 1985. The Economics of Pastoralism in Northern Kenya: The Rendille and the Gabra. *IPAL Technical Report F-3.* Nairobi: UNESCO.

Oxby, C. 1981. Group Ranches in Africa. *Overseas Development Institute Review* 2:44–56.

Perlov, D.C. 1983. The Role of Commercial Livestock in Samburu Economic Strategies—Research Notes. *Rural Africana* 15–16:127–130.

Phillipson, D.W. 1988. *African Archeology.* Cambridge: Cambridge University Press.

Pratt, D. J. and M. D. Gwynne (eds.) 1977. *Rangeland Management and Ecology in East Africa.* Huntington: Kreiger.

Rees, P.H., E.N. Mngola, P. O'Leary, and H.O. Pamba. 1974. Intestinal Parasites. IN L.C. Vogel, A.S.Muller, R.S.Odingo, Z.Onyango, and A. de Geus (eds.) *Health and Disease in Kenya*. Pp. 339–346. Nairobi: East Africa Literature Bureau.

Republic of Kenya 1984a. *Marsabit District Development Plan 1984/1988*. Nairobi: Ministry of Finance and Planning.

Republic of Kenya 1984b. *Turkana District Development Plan 1984/1988*. Nairobi: Ministry of Finance and Planning.

Republic of Kenya 1988. *Marsabit District Development Plan 1988/1992*. Nairobi: Ministry of Finance and Planning.

Rey, P. Ph. 1979. Class Contradiction in Lineage Societies. Critique of Anthropology, 13 and 14:41–60.

Richardson, K. 1968. *Garden of Miracles*. London: AIM-Victory Press.

Rigby, P. 1985. *Persistent Pastoralists*. London: ZED Publications.

Roth, E.A. 1991. Education, Tradition and Household Labor among Rendille Pastoralists in Northern Kenya. *Human Organization* 50:136–141.

Rutagwenda, T. 1985. The Control of Important Camel Diseases in the IPAL Study Area. *IPAL Technical Report No. E-7*, pp. 9–75. Nairobi: UNESCO Integrated Project in Arid Lands.

Sahlins, M.D. 1961. The Segmentary Lineage: An Organization of Predatory Expansion. *American Anthropologist* 63:322–345.

Salzman, P.C. 1971. Comparative Studies of Nomadic Pastoralism. *Anthropology Quarterly* 44(3).

Salzman, P. C. 1972. The Status of Nomadism as a Cultural Phenomenon in the Middle East. *Journal of Asian and African Studies* 8:60–68.

Salzman, P. C. 1980. Introduction: Processes of Sedenterization as Adaptation and Response. IN P. C. Salzman (ed.) *When Nomads Settle: Processes of Sedenterization as Adaptation and Response*, pp. 1–19. NY: J.F. Bergin Publishers, Inc.

Sato, S. 1980. Pastoral Movements and the Subsistence Unit of the Rendille of Northern Kenya. *Senri Ethnological Studies* 6:1–28. Osaka: National Museum of Ethnology.

Schmidt-Nielsen, K. 1964. *Desert Animals: Physiological Problems of Heat and Water*. Oxford: Clarendon Press.

Schwartz, H.J. 1979. The Transport Camel of the Rendille of Marsabit District, Kenya. IN W.R.Cockrill (ed.) *The Camelid* pp. 161–173. Uppsala: Scandinavian Institute of African Studies.

Schwartz, H.J. 1980a. An Introduction to the Livestock Ecology Programme. *IPAL Technical Report A-3* pp. 56–61. Nairobi: UNESCO Integrated Project in Arid Lands.

Schwartz, H.J. 1980b. *Draft Final Report: On the Implementation of the UNESCO-FRG Traditional Livestock Management Program*. June 1978–July 1980. Nairobi: UNESCO-IPAL.

Schwartz, S. and H.J. Schwartz 1985. Nomadic Pastoralism in Kenya—Still a Viable Production System? *Quarterly Journal of International Agriculture* 24(1):5–21.

Sen, A. K. 1981. *Poverty and Famines: An Essay on Entitlement and Deprivation*. Oxford: Clarendon Press.

Simpkin, S.P. 1985. The Effects of Diseases as Constraints to Camel Production in Northern Kenya. IN *IPAL Technical Report E-7* Pp. 78–160, Nairobi: UNESCO.

Sobania, N.W. 1979. Background History of the Mt. Kulal Region of Kenya. *IPAL Technical Report No. A-2*. Nairobi: UNESCO

Sobania, N.W. 1980a. *The Historical Tradition of the Peoples of the Eastern Lake Turkana Basin c. 1840–1925*. Ph.D. dissertation. University of London.

Sobania, N.W. 1980b. An Historical Study of Rendille Migration Patterns. IN H.J. Schwartz (ed.) *Draft Final Report: On the Implementation of the UNESCO-FRG Traditional Livestock Management Project June 1978–July 1980.*pp. 104–128. Nairobi: UNESCO-IPAL.

Sobania, N. W. 1988. Pastoralist Migration and Colonial Policy: A Case Study from Northern Kenya. IN D. Johnson and D. Anderson (eds.) *The Ecology of Survival: Case Studies from North East African History* pp. 219–239 London: Crook Greene.

Sobania, N. W. [In Press]. Defeat and Dispersal: The Laikipiak and their Neighbors in the 19th Century. IN T. Spear and R. Waller (eds.) *Being Maasai: Ethnicity and Identity in East Africa.* London: James Currey.

Spear, T. 1981. *Kenya's Past.* Essex: Longman Group.

Spear, T. [In Press]. Being Maasai. IN T. Spear and R. Waller (eds.) *Being Maasai: Ethnicity and Identity in East Africa.* London: James Currey.

Spencer, P. 1965. *The Samburu: A Study of Gerontocracy in a Nomadic Tribe.* Berkeley: University of California Press.

Spencer, P. 1973. *Nomads in Alliance.* London: Oxford University Press.

Spencer, P. 1976. Opposing Streams and the Gerontocratic Ladder: Two Models of Age-Organization in East Africa. *MAN (N.S.)* 11(2):153–74.

Sperling, L. 1987a. Food Acquisition During the African Drought of 1983–84: A Study of Kenyan Herders. *Disasters* 11(4):263–72.

Sperling, L. 1987b. Wage Employment Among Samburu Pastoralists of Northcentral Kenya. *Research in Economic Anthropology* 9:167–190.

Spooner, B. 1973. *The Cultural Ecology of Pastoral Nomads.* Addison-Wesley Module Anthropology No. 45. Reading, Mass: Addison-Wesley.

Stenning, D. 1959. *Savanna Nomads: A Study of the WoDaabe Pastoral Fulani of Western Bornu Province, Northern Region, Nigeria.* Oxford: Oxford University Press.

Sutton, J.E.G. 1973. The Settlement of East Africa. IN B.A. Ogot (ed.) *Zamani: A Survey of East African History,* New Edition, Pp. 70–97. Nairobi: Longman.

Swift, J. 1977. Sahelian Pastoralists: Underdevelopment, Desertification and Famine. *Annual Reviews of Anthropology* 6:457–78.

Timberlake, L. 1988. *Only One Earth: Living for the Future.* NY: Sterling Publ. Co., Inc.

Tonah, O.W. Steve. 1988 *Changes in a Pastoral Society: The Case of the Ariaal Rendille of Northern Kenya—Trading Activities and the Role of Traders.* Diplom. Thesis, Faculty of Sociology, University of Bielefeld.

UNEP 1977. *Desertification, Its Causes and Consequences. Proceedings of the United Nations Conference on Desertification.* Nairobi: United Nations Environment Programme.

Van Zwannenberg, R.M.A. 1977. *An Economic History of Kenya and Uganda 1800-1970.* London: MacMillan Press Ltd.

Vossen, R. 1978. Linguistic Evidence Regarding the Territorial History of the Maa-speaking Peoples: Some Preliminary Remarks. *Kenya Historical Review* 6:35–52.

Vossen, R. 1982. *The Eastern Nilotes: Linguistic and Historical Reconstructions.* Berlin: Dietrich Reimer Verlag.

Waller, R. 1978. *The Lords of East Africa: The Masai in the Mid-Nineteenth Century c. 1840-1888.* Ph.D. Dissertation Cambridge University.

Waller, R. 1985. Ecology Migration and Expansion in East Africa. *African Affairs* 84:347–70.

Waller, R. 1988. Emutai: Crisis and Response in Maasailand 1883–1902. IN D. Johnson and D. Anderson (eds.) *The Ecology of Survival,* pp. 73–112. London: Lester Crook Academic Publishing.

Western, D. 1982. The Environment and Ecology of Pastoralists in Arid Savannas. *Development and Change* 13:183–211.

Western, D. and V. Finch 1986. Cattle and Pastoralism: Survival and Production in Arid Lands. *Human Ecology* 14(1):77–94.

WHO 1965. *Technical Report 301.* Geneva: World Health Organization.

Wilson, A.J., R. Dolan, H.J. Schwartz, and C.R. Field 1979. Diseases of Camels in Kenya. IN W.R. Cockrill (ed.) *The Camelid.* Pp. 519–531. Uppsala: Scandinavian Institute of African Studies.

Wiseman, D.P. 1977. *Primary Health Care Project in Marsabit District.* Report Submitted to Ministry of Health, Republic of Kenya MCH/FP. Nairobi: Ministry of Health.

World Bank 1981. *Accelerated Development in Sub-Saharan Africa.* Washington D.C.: The World Bank.

World Bank, 1984. *Toward Sustained Development in Sub-sahara Africa: A joint Program of Action.* Washington D.C.: The World Bank.

World Bank, 1986. *Poverty and Hunger: Issues and Options for Food Security in Developing Countries.* Washington: D.C. The World Bank.

World Bank, 1990. *Poverty: World Development Report 1990.* Oxford: Oxford University Press. Bergin Publishers, Inc.

Index

T - #0269 - 081024 - C0 - 229/152/8 - PB - 9780367304737 - Gloss Lamination